11/20

A PECULIAR INDIFFERENCE

A PECULIAR INDIFFERENCE

THE NEGLECTED TOLL OF
VIOLENCE ON BLACK AMERICA

Elliott Currie

Metropolitan Books
Henry Holt and Company   New York

Metropolitan Books
Henry Holt and Company
Publishers since 1866
120 Broadway
New York, New York 10271
www.henryholt.com

Metropolitan Books® and m ® are registered trademarks of
Macmillan Publishing Group, LLC.

Library of Congress Cataloging-in-Publication Data

Names: Currie, Elliott, author.
Title: A peculiar indifference : the neglected toll of violence on black
    America / Elliott Currie.
Other titles: Neglected toll of violence on black America
Description: First edition. | New York : Metropolitan Books, Henry Holt and
    Company, 2020. | Includes bibliographical references and index.
Identifiers: LCCN 2020013956 (print) | LCCN 2020013957 (ebook) |
    ISBN 9781250769930 (hardcover) | ISBN 9781250769947 (ebook)
Subjects: LCSH: African Americans—Violence against—History—21st
    century. | African Americans—Social conditions—21st century. | African
    Americans—Economic conditions—21st century. | Race
    discrimination—United States—History—21st century. | Social
    justice—United States—History—21st century. | United States—Race
    relations—History—21st century.
Classification: LCC E185.615 .C87 2020 (print) | LCC E185.615 (ebook) |
    DDC 305.800973—dc23
LC record available at https://lccn.loc.gov/2020013956
LC ebook record available at https://lccn.loc.gov/2020013957

Our books may be purchased in bulk for promotional, educational, or business
use. Please contact your local bookseller or the Macmillan Corporate and
Premium Sales Department at (800) 221-7945, extension 5442, or
by e-mail at MacmillanSpecialMarkets@macmillan.com.

First Edition 2020

Designed by Kelly S. Too

Printed in the United States of America

1 3 5 7 9 10 8 6 4 2

CONTENTS

A PECULIAR INDIFFERENCE

AN ENDURING EMERGENCY

In early August 2018 I took a trip to Chicago, the city where I grew up. While I was there, the city suffered what newspapers described as one of its deadliest weekends in recent memory. Between 5:00 p.m. on Friday afternoon, August 3, and 6:00 a.m. on Monday, August 6, at least seventy-one people were shot in the city, of whom twelve died. Thirty of the victims were shot within a single three-hour period early Sunday morning.

The violence was overwhelmingly concentrated in a handful of neighborhoods on the city's South and West Sides. Eight people were shot at one block party in South Side's Gresham community alone. Anyone familiar with these neighborhoods would know that they are not strangers to this kind of violence, and that though the sheer amount of violence that week was unusual, its concentration in these particular places was not.[1]

The twelve people who died in the weekend's shootings ranged in age from seventeen to fifty-nine, and they were a diverse group in other ways as well. Several were young men with extensive criminal records who were gunned down in what appeared to be gang-related disputes. Twenty-six-year-old Kendall Brown, killed by shots from a passing Jeep on the South Side around 1:00 a.m. on Sunday, had been arrested fourteen times between August 2009 and April 2014, including five times for domestic battery and once for being a felon in possession of a firearm. Others were the victims of trivial conflicts that escalated into deadly confrontations. Seventeen-year-old Kenny Ivory was shot twice after getting into an argument with some other boys while riding his bicycle near his home in Gresham. Thirty-year-old Earl Young was with his fiancée at her South Side apartment when they got into an argument with a neighbor about her puppies "peeing from her third-floor balcony onto his below." The neighbor shot Earl in the back.[2]

Still other victims were simply in the wrong place at the wrong time. Fifty-nine-year-old contractor Frank Warren was taking a lunch break just before noon on Saturday, on the grass in front of a house where he was working on a pool deck, in South Side's Englewood community, when two men across the street began shooting at each other. Frank was hit twice in the abdomen and died shortly thereafter.[3] Seventeen-year-old Jahnae Patterson, the lone female homicide victim that weekend, was at a late-night block party in North Lawndale on the West Side with her three best friends. As the four girls walked down the street to use the bathroom, two men began firing toward people at the block party. Jahnae was hit multiple times; she tried to run away but collapsed and died in the doorway of a nearby apartment building. She had hoped to become a nurse and had planned to buy a house someday with Chinyere Jordan, one of the friends who'd gone with her to the block party. "She shouldn't have lost her life right here in front of everybody," Chinyere said afterward. "We weren't supposed to see that happen."[4]

There was a grim sense of déjà vu to some of the twelve killings. Fifty-year-old Ron Johnson, who was shot in the head not far from his home in the Altgeld Gardens neighborhood on the far South Side shortly after midnight on Monday morning, had just the day before gone to the funeral of one of his best friends—also shot to death in Altgeld Gardens.[5]

But though the twelve people killed over the weekend spanned a wide range of ages and social circumstances, almost all of them had one striking thing in common. With the sole exception of Frank Warren, the Englewood contractor, all were African American.[6] And as with the concentration of these deaths in certain neighborhoods, there was nothing new about that, either. Of the 564 killings in Chicago from August 2017 to August 2018, the race of the victim was recorded for 504. Of those 504 victims, 411 were African American, 49 were Hispanic, 43 were white, and one was Asian.[7] In the city as a whole, only

31 percent of the population is African American; roughly the same proportion is non-Hispanic white, 29 percent is Latino, and 6 percent Asian. African Americans, then, were less than a third of Chicago's population but more than 80 percent of its victims of homicide.[8] By contrast, non-Hispanic whites, also a third of the city's population, were only 9 percent of homicide victims.

The media, not only in Chicago but nationally, expressed predictable shock over this weekend of violence, and speculated over what it was about the city of Chicago in particular that could explain it. But while Chicago's homicide rate is very high—at 24 homicides per 100,000 people in 2017, it was roughly four times the rate for the country as a whole—it is routinely outpaced by that of many other American cities. Two cities just a stone's throw from Chicago—St. Louis, Missouri, and Gary, Indiana—racked up homicide rates in 2017 that were well over two and a half times Chicago's. Across the Mississippi River from St. Louis, meanwhile, the perennially violence-torn small city of East St. Louis, Illinois, achieved a homicide rate of 111 per 100,000—close to five times Chicago's rate of violent death.[9]

And in Chicago, as in all of these cities, violence has stalked the streets and homes for a long time. The city actually suffered its worst year for homicide in 1974, and though the numbers have fluctuated since then, there has never been a time in recent history that Chicago (or St. Louis, or New Orleans, or Detroit, or Baltimore) has not experienced levels of violent death that are otherwise seen only in the most violent countries of the developing world.[10] And in every one of those cities, black Americans have been dramatically overrepresented among the victims.

In response to the especially deadly August weekend, Chicago's police superintendent rushed to insist that "this is not a widespread issue among citizens of this city. This is a small subset of individuals who think they can play by their own rules because they continue to get a slap on the wrist when we arrest them."[11] The problem, he said, was that those who engaged in violence were not being held to account for their actions. "I hear people holding [the police] accountable all the time," he said. "I never hear people saying those individuals out here on the streets need to stop pulling the trigger." Those people, the superintendent concluded, "get a free pass from everybody, and they shouldn't." Chicago's then mayor, Rahm Emanuel, called for an "attitudinal change" in the city. "This might not be politically correct," he opined, "but I know the power of what faith and family can do." A local city alderman said that it was up to "the community" to step up to put an end to the violence. The city promised to deploy an extra 430 police officers to the hardest-hit neighborhoods. When, despite the greatly increased police deployment, the city suffered another sixty shootings the following weekend, the police superintendent again reassured residents that the violence did not reflect anything about Chicago itself but only represented the actions of a "small element."[12] The following year, after two only slightly less deadly weekends—fifty-two shootings and eight deaths in the first

weekend in June 2019, fifty-nine shot and seven killed over
the first weekend in August—the response was not much
different.[13]

And there was nothing new about this essentially eva-
sive response, either. In Chicago, as in every other American city where violence is endemic, sudden flare-ups
typically bring an initial flurry of outrage, sincere expressions of anger—usually directed at that "small element"
who are seen as mainly responsible—and then a waning
of interest. Not much is done to deal with the underlying
problem, and the city goes back, at least for a while, to
life as usual. Most of the time, in most places, violence in
the black community doesn't make the headlines or even
rate a mention on nighttime TV. For most people who
live outside the most stricken communities, deadly violence is just part of the background noise of contemporary
American urban life, something that happens in "bad"
neighborhoods—neighborhoods that are not theirs. That
kind of complacency is harder to find in communities like
North Lawndale or Englewood. But the people who live
in those places usually have relatively little voice and even
less political influence, which both serves to cover over the
everyday violence that surrounds them and to ensure that
the deeper conditions that cause it remain mostly unaddressed.

The result is that America continues to tolerate one of the
most fundamental inequalities imaginable: a radical disparity in the very prospect of survival itself. And we tolerate it
despite the fact that disparities in violence on this scale have

been, for all practical purposes, eliminated in every other advanced industrial society. Other wealthy countries, to be sure, also have racial and ethnic differences in the risks of violent death and injury, but none come even close to the level of excess mortality, disability, and suffering that we have come to tacitly accept as part of the American landscape. And those stark gaps in the risks of violence do not stand alone: they are only one particularly glaring example of a much broader pattern of systemic racial inequalities in health and well-being that sets the United States off sharply from every other advanced nation in the world.[14]

In the United States today, a young black man has fifteen times the chances of dying from violence as his white counterpart. Violence takes more years of life from black men than cancer, stroke, and diabetes combined. It strikes even black women more often than white men and contributes significantly to persistently lower overall life expectancy and higher infant mortality among black Americans.[15] These disparities contribute to sharply divergent overall patterns of life and death between whites and blacks in the United States. Yet aside from spectacular incidents like Chicago's deadly summer weekends, they have largely receded into the background of public discussion and have very nearly disappeared as a target of public policy. It is hard to believe that the country would have the same tepid response if the racial distribution of violence were reversed. If young white men had the same homicide death rate as their African American counterparts do now, roughly 14,000 of them would have been victims of homicide in 2018, instead of the 930 who actually were. I think it is safe to say that if 14,000 young white men were dying of violence in the United States every year, it would be considered a problem calling for urgent attention, with resources to match.

Much of the country has been understandably outraged by the continuing plague of police killings of black Americans; after the death of George Floyd at the hands of Minneapolis police in May 2020, that anger exploded into some of the most widespread and sustained protests against police violence in US history. There has been far less outrage over the ongoing emergency of everyday interpersonal violence in black communities. But it is important to understand that both of these kinds of violence are closely related aspects of the overall environment of danger that exists in too many black neighborhoods and that both are bred by the same underlying conditions: the continuing marginality, neglect, and structural disadvantage those neighborhoods face. We find it easier to understand this connection when the hand that holds the gun that kills a young black man is that of a white police officer. When the hand belongs to another young black man, the connection is less direct and less transparent. But it is no less real. Our inability or unwillingness to recognize that connection represents a failure of the moral as well as the sociological imagination and helps to perpetuate a level of preventable trauma and needless suffering that has no counterpart anywhere in the developed world.

This book is about the extent, consequences, and causes of that suffering and about what it would take to end it. It has been hard for us, as a society, to face up to the reality of racial disparities in violence. Many people are anxious at the prospect of talking directly about these sensitive issues, afraid that even to bring them up will play into long-standing stereotypes about black people and crime. And the anxiety is understandable. The stereotypes are pervasive, and there is no shortage of people who are ready to use them in the service of racist and regressive social policies. For some, that is reason enough to bury the subject of race and violence as a focus of dialogue and social action. But while I understand and respect those fears, I can't agree with the conclusion. Denial and avoidance can't be our response to an ongoing public health crisis of devastating proportions. The stakes are simply too high. Violence not only takes a huge toll of lives in black America; it also reverberates beyond the immediate victims to undermine the quality of life of whole communities. And in the absence of serious intervention, it will continue to do so. That is not an outcome we should be willing to accept.

An open reckoning with the roots of this crisis is especially urgent because what is already a devastating problem could well get worse. As I write, Donald Trump's presidential administration is vigorously pursuing policies at the national level that seem almost designed to exacerbate racial disparities in the risks of violent death and injury—policies that aim to reduce already meager public support for people living in low-income communities and to deepen their social and economic marginalization. Those policies, if carried out, will adversely affect Americans of all races but will hit black Americans especially hard. No one can predict the impact this will have on levels of violence in America's communities, but it would be foolish to ignore the danger that these policies represent.[16]

Our response should not be to deny the reality of this emergency but to confront it openly—and to link it firmly to its real causes. Part of the reluctance to talk directly about high levels of violence in some black communities stems from the fear that the problem will be blamed on supposed inherent failings of black Americans themselves. But more than a century's worth of careful research shows that the racial disparity in violence is not a symptom of community failure: it is a symptom of social injustice. And though that injustice is long-standing, it is also both preventable and reversible. Taking on this emergency with the seriousness it deserves requires that we understand its scope, consequences, and causes and that we think through what the evidence tells us about what needs to be done.

This book aims to contribute to that understanding. It is not meant to be a textbook or comprehensive academic treatise, or an original research monograph. It is an argument about why our stark racial disparities in violence exist and what strategies to combat them hold the most promise: an argument grounded in what is now a vast amount of research from many disciplines—criminology, sociology, psychology, public health, emergency medicine, and more. Much of that research is illuminating and important, but most of it never reaches a broad audience. My hope is that this book will help to both inform that wider audience about the depth and consequences of the racial violence divide and stimulate long-overdue social action to address its causes. We know a great deal about the sources of this enduring crisis and what it would take to end it. The problem is that we have failed to act on what we know.

I focus almost entirely on racial disparities in violent death and injury between black and white Americans—not because the experience of other groups is unimportant, but just the opposite. Stubbornly high rates of violent death and injury can be found, to varying degrees, in many communities, including white, Latino, Native American, and Asian. But all of these experiences are distinct, and we cannot do justice to any of them if we try to lump them together and examine them through a single lens. One of the main arguments in this book, indeed, is that the historical and contemporary experience of African Americans is profoundly different from that of other racial and ethnic groups and that we cannot fully understand their experience of violence without situating it within that unique context.

The following chapters describe the dimensions of the racial violence divide and its multiple impacts on communities, explore the long history of attempts to explain its social and economic roots, and point to some of the elements of a solution. Chapter 1 sketches the magnitude of the racial disparities in violence in the United States, exploring the patterns of both violent death and the far more common nonfatal (but often disabling) violence. I draw on a wealth of data and recent research in public health, criminology, and other disciplines to chart the extraordinary level of violence suffered by young black men in America, which puts them among the people at highest risk of violent death and injury anywhere in the world. But I also highlight the special vulnerability of black women and children—showing that the impact of racial disparities is so great that it often confounds our expectations about the relationships among gender, age, and the risks of violence. The evidence also strongly challenges two common but deeply misleading perceptions: that violence has become a relatively minor issue in the United States since the "crime drop" of the 1990s, and that we have arrived at a "color-blind" society in which opportunities and life conditions have become more and more indistinguishable between the races.

The consequences of concentrated violence do not end with the immediate damage done to the lives, bodies, and spirits of individual victims. Chapter 2 shows that in the most stricken communities, violence shapes and diminishes the quality of life in many ways—some of which, in a vicious cycle, work to perpetuate more violence in the future. I explore a fast-growing body of research, from public health, psychology, criminology, and other fields, showing that high levels of violence affect everything from the way parents raise their children to young people's educational attainment, from mental and physical health to expectations for the future. These impacts are sometimes subtle and complex, but they are an integral aspect of the radically different experience of violence between black and white Americans.

In chapters 3 and 4, I delve into the rich and varied literature that seeks to explain the sources of that difference— a literature that stretches back well over a hundred years.

Chapter 3 begins with the work of the great African American scholar and activist W.E.B. Du Bois, whose book *The Philadelphia Negro* contains some of the earliest (and still most trenchant) analysis of the roots of urban violence in black America. It moves on to consider some important analyses of race and violence in the mid-twentieth century, including classic investigations of Southern black communities in the 1930s, the monumental project that culminated in Gunnar Myrdal's enormously influential book *An American Dilemma* in the 1940s, and the pioneering work of the social psychologist Kenneth Clark on the "Dark Ghetto" of the urban North in the 1960s. I argue that despite some differences of perspective and emphasis, there was a remarkable degree of agreement among these writers about both the structural roots of racial disparities in violence and the strategies needed to confront them. All of them acknowledged the seriousness of the problem of violence in many black communities but also firmly connected it to the destructive impact of the specific history of racial oppression in America—a uniquely severe system of economic and political disadvantage that had inflicted pervasive harm on community life and personality. Though often overlooked today, this pioneering body of work remains vitally important—not only because it is a rich trove of insights on race and violence in America's past, but because many of those insights, and the strategic ideas that flowed from them, remain fresh and relevant. Our failure to heed them, indeed, helps to explain why we have made so little headway against racialized violence thus far.

Chapter 4 brings the analysis up to the present. Since the 1980s, there has been an explosion of research on racial disparities in violence, much of which is specialized and often highly technical. This chapter makes no attempt to cover the entirety of that research but sifts out some of its most important findings and highlights their implications for social action. I argue that beneath the formidable complexity of much of this research, there is a remarkably consistent set of conclusions that, in all essential respects, upholds the perspective of the pioneering scholars of race and violence. Despite some controversy at the margins and disagreements on the specifics, the contemporary research hammers home those scholars' core understanding: the high levels of violence that plague some African American communities are rooted in uniquely adverse structural conditions that are amplified by the enduring legacy of segregation and discrimination. And the latest research confirms the scope and depth of the social and personal harm that racial inequality continues to inflict in an era that is sometimes described as "color-blind."

The very fact that we are still doing this kind of research is a sign of our national failure to address the roots of that harm. But the research is more than a record of failure: it also provides clues to the path forward. The evidence described in those two chapters points unambiguously to the key elements of a strategy for change. Many of those elements have been understood for generations. Yet our national response, with some notable exceptions, has consistently failed to make use of that knowledge. Chapter 5 argues that it is past time that we change direction and, finally, begin to tackle the long-standing structural roots of violence. Rather than presenting a simple "laundry list" of potentially helpful programs and policies, I focus on several core elements that I believe must be central in an effective strategy to put an end to the racial violence divide. Chief among them is public investment to strengthen the essential institutions of care, nurturance, and opportunity that all communities need in order to thrive but that have been systematically withheld—or stripped—from parts of black America. That means a commitment to guaranteeing meaningful work and to rebuilding a capable and nurturing public sector in education, health care, and crucial public services. A serious strategy against endemic violence will also require a more responsible gun policy and a fundamental rethinking of the way we approach preventive and rehabilitative work with the most vulnerable youth. And I argue that we will also need to roll back America's disastrous investment in punitive control of black communities—a harsh and exclusionary strategy that has drained critical public resources and compounded the obstacles those communities face, while demonstrably failing to put an end to endemic violence.

Chapter 5 affirms the book's central message—that the persistence of extreme levels of violent death and injury in one of the world's wealthiest and most productive societies is a sign of a profound social failure. But it also shows that this failure is preventable. For more than a century, we have, in all important respects, known what is wrong and, at least in broad terms, what to do. At bottom, those disparities endure not because we do not understand them or because we are powerless to deal with them but because we—at least those of us with the capacity to effectively influence social, economic, and political decisions—have chosen again and again to allow them to persist.

Some readers may find the chapter's proposals to be unrealistically ambitious. But I believe they are the ones that are most clearly supported by the evidence, and I do not think that anything less will suffice to put an end to this most egregious of racial injustices. It won't be easy, but part of our problem has been the tendency to look for an easy solution at the expense of the solution that will actually work—to grasp at some new youth program or police tactic as if it will somehow overcome the effects of generations of exploitation and dispossession and the absence of solid paths to a more secure and just future. It hasn't happened, and it won't.

The book's title is taken from W.E.B. Du Bois, who, speaking of the country's attitude toward the well-being of black Americans generally, wrote at the close of the nineteenth century that there had been "few other cases in the history of civilized peoples where human suffering has been viewed with such peculiar indifference."[17] When it comes to the violence that afflicts black communities, a peculiar indifference still shapes our twenty-first-century response. This emergency persists for a tangle of intertwined reasons: the economic dispensability of poor Americans of all races in an increasingly heedless global economy; the fact that the communities that suffer violence the most are those with the least voice or influence in the political arena; the spread of a punitive and austere culture that has shaped crucial decisions about the allocation of social resources in ways that have damaged low-income people across the board, but African Americans especially. The racial violence divide, like other long-standing racial disparities in health and well-being, is not an inevitable fact of urban life or the result of abstract economic or technological forces. It is not a reflection of biological or cultural deficiencies. It is the result of conscious decisions that, while systematically impoverishing some communities, have helped to create extraordinary privilege and wealth in others. That wealth gives us both the means and the responsibility to reverse the consequences of those decisions. Our failure to do so—our peculiar indifference—is not only socially destructive and economically wasteful but a profound moral default.

ONE

DIMENSIONS

The epidemic of Ebola that struck several West African countries in 2014 drew an enormous amount of attention and concern around the world—and a collective sense of relief when it was officially declared to be over two years later. According to the World Health Organization, about eleven thousand people died in this outbreak of one of the world's deadliest diseases in the three hardest-hit countries: Sierra Leone, Guinea, and Liberia. That is a lot of people.[1] But it is less than the number of African Americans who die from homicide every eighteen months in the United States.

Between 2000 and 2018, the most recent data available, more than 162,000 black Americans lost their lives to violence.[2] To put that very abstract number into some perspective, imagine that we had lined up the entire population of a substantial midsize American city—say, Jackson, Mississippi—and mowed them down mercilessly, killing every man, woman, and child. And bear in mind that those deaths took place after the much vaunted "crime drop" of the 1990s, at a time when it was often said that violent crime was not the problem it used to be.

The figure of about 162,000 deaths over eighteen years translates into an average annual homicide death *rate* for the African American population as a whole of just under 20 per 100,000 people. Again, that number, by itself, may seem too abstract to mean much—until we compare it with the rate for whites. For white Americans (more precisely, for what the US Census Bureau calls "white non-Hispanic" Americans), the rate was about 2.8 per 100,000 during those years. The overall homicide death rate for black Americans since the start of the twenty-first century, then, has averaged seven times that of white Americans.

Among men, the black/white disparity in homicide rates is more than nine to one. For *young* men—those aged fifteen to twenty-nine—it is sixteen to one. Among women that age, the disparity is less severe: a young black woman is "only" four times more likely to be a victim of homicide than a white one.

I

Those disparities may seem shocking, but they are only the tip of the iceberg. For instance, the link between race and

violence in America is sufficiently powerful that it over-
turns some of our usual expectations about where violence
strikes hardest. One of those expectations has to do with
gender; another, with age.

Consider gender first. It is a truism in criminology that
homicide usually strikes men far more often than women—
especially in societies that, like the United States, have
high rates of homicide overall. And when we look at how
violent death has played out in recent years *within* different racial groups, that expectation holds. Among those
162,000 black Americans who died by homicide during
the first years of the twenty-first century, about 139,000—
85 percent of them—were male. The violent death rate
among black men during this period has averaged six times
that of black women. But so strong is the effect of race that
a black *woman* has half again as much a chance of dying by
homicide as a white *man*.

Now consider age. In the United States, as in many other
societies that have high levels of violence, it is the young
who suffer it the most. And as with the gender disparity,
that relationship holds true in the United States *within*
every racial group. More than half of all homicide deaths
among black men in America take place among those aged
fifteen to twenty-nine. The person with the greatest likelihood of dying by violence in the United States in 2018
was a twenty-three-year-old black man; among whites, a
thirty-year-old man. The chance that a man will die of
homicide starts to rise in his teens, peaks in the twenties to
early thirties for both races (somewhat later for whites than

blacks), and then begins a long slide downward as they move into middle age and beyond. So age matters—and it matters a lot. But once again, race matters even more, overriding the age effect. A *sixty-year-old* black man remains three times as likely to suffer a violent death as a white man of thirty (which, again, was the age of *highest* risk for white men in America in 2018).

What makes these disparities even more sobering is that the rates of violent death for *white* men in the United States are themselves quite high by comparison with those of men in other advanced industrial societies. Put up against men in, say, Japan, Germany, England, or Australia, white men in the United States—especially young white men—are a distinctly vulnerable group. They are several times more likely to meet a violent death than men of all races combined in other countries at comparable levels of economic development. The current annual homicide death rate for non-Hispanic white men in the United States, at nearly 4 per 100,000, is more than five times the rate for all German men, and close to twenty times the rate for men in Japan.[3] So when we say that a black man in America is nine times as likely to die by violence as his white counterpart, we are comparing him with people whose risk of being murdered is itself unusually high in the developed world.[4]

And these numbers are averages, for the United States as a whole. In many places in America, the racialized presence of violent death looms much larger than that. In the state of Illinois, for instance, the homicide death rate for young

African American men (ages fifteen to twenty-nine) has averaged 143 per 100,000 over the course of the twenty-first century, thirty-seven times the rate for white men the same age.[5] Homicide death rates this high are unknown virtually anywhere else on the planet. You can find them in some parts of Mexico and Central America. You can find them in some cities in Brazil. You can find them in some places in southern Africa. You will not find them in any other advanced industrial society—not even close.

Of the world's fifty most violent large cities, as measured by their homicide death rate, only four are outside the global South—and all four are in the United States. In 2017, St. Louis, Missouri, reached number thirteen on the list; Baltimore was twenty-first, with New Orleans and Detroit at forty-one and forty-two, respectively. The homicide rate in St. Louis, at 66 per 100,000, was exceeded in only twelve major cities anywhere in the world—six in Mexico, four in Brazil, and two in Venezuela. The Missouri city beat out places like San Salvador, El Salvador; Cali, Colombia; Ciudad Juárez, Mexico; Guatemala City, Guatemala; and Recife, Brazil—all among the most notoriously violent cities in the most violent countries of the global South.[6] And the American cities that make this list are invariably disproportionately black and disproportionately poor. Blacks make up about 13 percent of the national population in the United States but are roughly half the population in St. Louis, over 60 percent in Baltimore, and more than 80 percent in Detroit. They are fully 98 percent of the population of East St. Louis, Illinois—a city too small to be included on this international list but which suffers the highest homicide rate in the United States.[7]

What is perhaps most troubling is that these cities— along with others like Gary, Indiana, and Camden, New Jersey—have jockeyed for the top position in this grim ranking for years. In some cases, their high homicide figures represent declines from even worse rates in the recent past. In others, they reflect a discouraging stability or even increase in the level of death by violence. Baltimore's homicide rate in 2017, for example, was the highest in the city's history.[8]

Looking at violent death within cites as a whole, moreover, obscures its concentration in specific communities within them. A recent study of homicide trends in St. Louis found that from 2004 to 2016, the most dangerous census tract in the city racked up a total of 73 homicides—in an area encompassing only three-fifths of a square mile, with fewer than 5,000 residents at the end of the study period. The tract's 2016 homicide death rate of 140 per 100,000 was double the overall rate for St. Louis as a whole.[9]

Nationally, roughly three-fourths of homicides are committed with firearms, and we cannot understand violent death in America without confronting the outsize role of guns. But as with gender and age, race shapes and complicates this connection in revealing ways.

Gun homicides are a much bigger proportion of overall violent deaths among blacks than among whites—roughly 83 percent and 60 percent, respectively. That difference is mainly driven by the stunningly high rates of firearm homicide among black men, which, in 2018, were twelve times those of white men. Young black men in particular face a level of firearm homicide that is among the highest in the world—and for those with little formal education, one that exceeds the risk faced by the most vulnerable young men in the most violent countries of Latin America. A study of firearm mortality in four countries with extreme levels of gun violence—the United States, Mexico, Colombia, and Brazil—found that the rate of violent gun death among black men aged fifteen to thirty-four in the United States with a high school education or less was not only fourteen times the rate for similarly educated American white men but was also triple the rate for comparably educated black men in Brazil.[10]

But it is also important to understand that violent death is so prevalent among black men that their rate of death from *non*-firearm homicides is double whites' rate of death by firearm homicide. American men of both races are more likely to be killed with a gun than anything else, but a white man's chance of being killed with a gun remains less than a black man's chance of being killed without one.

II

When we think about violent death in America, the image that most likely comes to mind is the urban violence of the street—young men killing each other, usually with guns, in gang disputes or drug rivalries. And that kind of violence does account for a very substantial proportion of the racial disparity in homicide in America. But it is not the whole story. Focusing on street violence alone obscures the vast amount of violence that takes place within intimate relationships: between parents and children, between husbands and wives, between dating partners. Here, too, the pattern of racial disparity is stark.

A study of child abuse fatalities among American children from birth to age four, carried out by researchers from the Harvard and University of Pennsylvania medical schools, concluded that African American children—who make up only 16 percent of the nation's child population—were 37 percent of those who died of physical child abuse between 1999 and 2014. That translates into a death rate for African American children triple that for whites. (Notably, in this study, the category of "white" included both non-Hispanic and Hispanic whites, which lessens the magnitude of the disparity between non-Hispanic whites and African Americans.) The study was designed to test whether the chance that children would die of physical abuse was related to the level of poverty in the county where they lived. The answer was yes: counties with the highest poverty rates had by far the highest rates of fatal child abuse. But race once again upended this straightforward relationship. Black children living in counties with the lowest poverty rates were far more likely to die than white children in the counties with the *highest* poverty rates.[11]

These differences help account for the deep and long-standing racial disparities in overall infant mortality in the United States. In an analysis of infant deaths in Michigan between 1989 and 2005, researchers from Columbia University's School of Public Health noted that the death rate for black infants under a year old was around three times that of non-Hispanic whites. Much of that disparity could be explained by the fact that black mothers were more often subject to several conditions that tend to increase infant mortality for all races—including being younger when their children were born, having lower levels of education, and having limited access to adequate prenatal care. But even when these were accounted for, children of black mothers were half again as likely as whites to die violently before their first birthday.[12]

Race skews the rates of violence within adult relationships, too. Women of any race are far more likely to be killed by current or former partners than men are; intimate partner violence accounts for nearly half of the homicides of women in the United States. So it isn't surprising that such relationship-related violence makes a heavy contribution to black women's disproportionate risk of violent death.[13] A recent analysis of data from the Centers for Disease Control and Prevention, which examined over six thousand intimate partner homicides (almost all of them in opposite-sex pairings) from 2003 to 2015, found that black women were sharply overrepresented among female victims, accounting for 28 percent of the total. What may be more surprising, though, is that intimate partner violence also contributes to the excess risk faced by black men. Among the male victims—a smaller but still significant group, accounting for almost thirteen hundred homicides in the CDC data— the racial imbalance was even more striking than among female ones: nearly half of the men who died in these incidents of intimate partner violence were black.[14]

III

The excess risk of violent death for black Americans, in short, affects many groups we may not immediately think of as being uniquely vulnerable: black women as well as black men, older black men as well as younger ones, small children as well as adolescents and young adults. This extra risk is not subtle, and it is not just a matter of degree. It reflects a fundamental division in the quality of life that people of different races get to enjoy. And we can see this division even more clearly if we look at it through some other lenses.

For example, the strikingly high homicide death rates among blacks mean that the hierarchy of *causes* of death looks remarkably different between the races. People die, of course, for all kinds of reasons. But the way in which those reasons stack up tells us a lot about the kinds of lives that different groups lead and the kinds of hazards that they routinely face. Looking at racial differences in causes of death, accordingly, provides a useful perspective on the human meaning of racial inequality.[15]

For the United States population as a whole, homicide is the sixteenth most frequent cause of death, a ranking high enough to distinguish us from every other advanced industrial country. But that overall figure, as usual, masks sharply different experiences among the races. For blacks, violence is number eight on the list of major causes of death; for non-Hispanic whites, it is number twenty. For black men specifically, violence is the fifth leading cause of death—exceeded only by heart disease, cancer, unintentional injuries, and stroke. Homicide becomes the *leading* cause of death for black males beginning at age fifteen, and continues as their number one cause of death until age thirty. Among non-Hispanic white men, on the other hand, violence ranks eighteenth among causes of death, and homicide is *never* the leading cause of death for them at any age. Considerably fewer white men die of homicide than of aortic aneurisms or benign neoplasms.

And when we say that homicide is the leading cause of death among young black men, we are not saying that it edges out other causes: we are saying that it overwhelms them. Homicide accounts for almost half of all deaths among black men aged fifteen to twenty-four; more black men that age die of homicide than of the next nineteen biggest causes of death *combined*. Among white men in that age group, on the other hand, homicide accounts for just under 5 percent of deaths.

But even these numbers understate the human impact of violent death in many black communities. We can better appreciate that impact by using still another measure: what public health researchers call "years of potential life lost," or YPLL. YPLL is a measure of *premature* death. We choose an endpoint—say, age sixty-five—and ask how many years of life are lost before that age from a particular cause of death. YPLL, then, fuses two important but distinct factors: how widespread the cause of death is—how many people die of it—and how old they are when they die.

In the United States today, heart disease is the leading single *cause* of death: that is, more people ultimately die of it than of any other cause. But it is not the leading source of years of potential life lost—because people tend to die of heart disease at relatively older ages, thus losing fewer "potential" years of life when they do die. Instead, the biggest culprit for YPLL is what public health statisticians call "unintentional injuries"—a broad category that includes accidents, notably motor vehicle accidents, and "poisoning," which includes drug overdose deaths.

Since unintentional injuries typically happen earlier in life, they take a much bigger toll in years of potential life lost. If I die at sixty-three of a heart attack, then I have lost two years of potential life before age sixty-five. If I die at age fifteen in a car accident, I have lost fifty years of potential life. And that explains why, for the population as a whole, unintentional injuries are the biggest single source of years of potential life lost before age sixty-five.

This measure becomes very important in understanding the social and personal burden of violence in the United States, because violence—like accidents—strikes hardest at younger people. Since the highest risk of dying by violence in the United States is found among people from their late teens to their early thirties, the impact of homicide on YPLL is unusually high. Homicide, again, is the sixteenth leading cause of death among the population as a whole, but it is the sixth biggest cause of years of potential life lost before sixty-five.[16]

And seen through this lens, the racial disparities in the impact of violent death loom even larger. Though blacks are just 13 percent of the US population, they account for over half of all years of life lost to violence in the twenty-first century. For black men, homicide is the *leading* cause of years of life lost before age sixty-five. For white men, it ranks eighth. About one out of every six years of life that black men lose prematurely before age sixty-five is lost to violence. For white men, that figure is one in forty-five.

And when it comes to years of life lost, the racial effect once again overwhelms the standard expectations about gender. Gender, as usual, does make a big difference—up to a point. Black women lose far fewer years of life to violence than black men. But whereas, as I've noted, only about one in forty-five years of life lost prematurely among white men is lost to violence, for black women the proportion is twice that—one in twenty-three. Measured this way, by how many years of their lives it steals, violence looms much larger in the lives of black women than in the lives of white men. Black women lose far more years of life to homicide than to diabetes—a notorious killer of African American women.

The YPLL measure also helps us to grasp the extent of *police* violence in black communities. The homicide figures presented so far do not include deaths due to what the CDC calls "legal intervention," and it is widely believed that the official data on deaths due to police violence seriously understate them. But recent studies using other sources of data reveal both the extent of the problem and its racial concentration. One study, for example, finds about fifty-six thousand years of potential life lost each year to police violence, with blacks losing those years at a rate nearly three times that of whites.[17]

Statistics are a cold and in many ways inadequate tool for understanding the human impact of violence. But what we see here through the lens of YPLL is nothing less than a massive eradication of human potential. The data tell us something more than the simple fact that violent death strikes black Americans more frequently. They tell us that, because it strikes so often at the young, it erases a substantial part of the future of an entire community. The 162,000 homicides of black Americans in 2000–2018 stole an average of thirty-five years of life from each of their victims— roughly nine more years than are lost on average by white homicide victims, because blacks tend to lose their lives to violence at younger ages than whites. Those are years in which they otherwise could have married, had children, and voted; could have become teachers, firefighters, doctors, artists, or professors; could have become uncles, aunts, grandparents, and mentors.

IV

I have focused just on homicide so far, because it is both the most serious and the most reliably measurable form of violence. But far more Americans, of all races, are victims of violence that stops short of killing them. For every violent death in the United States, there are roughly ninety other violent assaults that send the victim to a hospital emergency room. Not all of that nonfatal violence is equally serious. But all too often, it has a long-term impact on the victims' health and emotional well-being; at worst, it can leave them seriously disabled. And it tends to be self-perpetuating: those who suffer violence once face a heightened risk of both suffering it again, sometimes fatally, and using violence themselves against others.

Often, too, the difference between fatal and nonfatal violence is little more than a matter of chance. As a growing body of research suggests, increasing numbers of victims of violent assaults who survive today would have died a generation ago, or even just a decade ago—not because of any changes in the intent or severity of the violence but simply because the medical community has gotten increasingly better at keeping people alive.[18] Since the difference between a fatal assault and a serious but nonfatal one may hinge on something as arbitrary as the accuracy of a shooter's aim, on how quickly an ambulance arrives on the scene, or on the distance to a well-equipped trauma center, it is not surprising that the distribution of serious but nonfatal violence closely resembles that of homicide. And in both cases, the pattern is unambiguous. Whether fatal or nonfatal, violence is not an equal opportunity affliction.

Nonfatal violence is harder to measure than homicide, and much of it escapes our conventional methods of gathering data. Crime statistics based on reports to police dramatically understate its prevalence, mainly because so many victims do not report it. That is especially true for two kinds of violence that make up a very large part of the total: violence suffered by people who are themselves involved in something illegal, such as gang youth or those in the drug trade; and intimate partner violence, whose victims may feel that telling police about their situation won't make it any better and might well make it worse. Those problems are likely to be exacerbated in poor communities of color, where trust in the police is often thin to nonexistent. Surveys of crime victims, which are sometimes thought to be more reliable because they don't depend on victims' willingness to talk to the police, also underestimate the extent of nonfatal violence, particularly because they tend to exclude many of the people who are most likely to suffer it—including street youth, the homeless, and people on the margins of society generally.[19]

Better evidence comes from medical statistics—especially data on admission to hospital emergency rooms, which minimize, though they do not eliminate, some of the limitations of other measures. Although even some people who are seriously injured in an assault do not seek medical treatment, often for the same reasons they do not report to the police, most do; and the more serious the injury, the more likely the victim is to show up at an emergency room.

National-level data on admissions to hospital emergency rooms, accordingly, can give us a broad initial sketch of the racial divide in nonfatal violence. According to CDC estimates, from 2001 through 2017 there were more than 28 million visits to an emergency room for an assault-related injury in the United States.[20] In about 6 million of them, the victim's race was not recorded. Of those where race is known, roughly 7.5 million of the victims were black, while about 10.4 million were non-Hispanic white. Thus, where race was known, the overall number of admissions for assault-related injuries was only about 38 percent higher for whites than for blacks, even though the non-Hispanic white population in the United States was nearly five times larger than the black population during this time.

If we look specifically at gun assaults—which tend to be among the most physically and emotionally damaging of nonfatal injuries—the racial imbalance widens dramatically. From 2001 through 2017, well over 400,000 African Americans were treated in an emergency room for a nonfatal firearm assault, versus roughly 122,000 whites. That disparity is so wide that even if all of the cases where the race of the victim is unknown were added into the white figure—which is thoroughly implausible—there would still have been over 50,000 more black than white victims in this period admitted to emergency rooms due to gun violence, despite the fact that the white population as a whole was nearly five times larger.

But just as with fatal violence, the racial disparity in nonfatal violence is not confined to guns. Assaults with knives and other sharp instruments are typically not as deadly as those committed with firearms, which is why guns loom so large in the figures on homicide. But they are much more common: from 2001 through 2017, more than twice as many Americans went to an emergency room for what the CDC calls "cut/pierce" assaults as for gunshot wounds. And of the nearly 1.7 million cut/pierce victims whose race was recorded, 45 percent were black, while just 31 percent were non-Hispanic whites—again, despite the nearly fivefold larger white population.

It is not gun violence alone, then, that sharply separates the races in America. It is, more generally, *serious* violence—usually committed with some kind of deadly weapon, and often life-threatening, or at the very least life-changing.

The broad national outline sketched by the CDC data is filled in by finer-grained studies that examine the racial distribution of violence on the state and local levels. In a study of hospital and emergency room admissions during the year 2010 in six states—Arizona, California, Maryland, New Jersey, North Carolina, and Wisconsin—researchers from the Urban Institute found that although the states differed considerably in the rates at which people went to the hospital for a firearm assault injury, stark racial disparities were present in all of them. Among young men aged fifteen to thirty-four, the rate of hospital visits for gun assaults among blacks was four times the rate among whites in Arizona, fifteen times the white rate in North Carolina, and seventeen times in California. In Wisconsin, the disparity was seventy-five to one; in New Jersey, a stunning ninety-eight to one. Among young women, the disparity between black and white ranged from a low of roughly eight to one in Arizona to a high of fifty-five to one in Wisconsin. And in every state except Arizona, the rate for young black *women* was higher than the rate for young white *men*—sometimes much higher: two and a half times higher in California, three times in Maryland, five times in Wisconsin, and over six times in New Jersey.[21]

The evidence also tells us that these extreme disparities are not going away. Looking at national-level data on hospital admissions for children under sixteen, for example, a group of Boston University and Columbia University researchers found that black children were more than four times as likely as whites to be hospitalized for gunshot injuries. They were less likely than whites to be hospitalized for self-inflicted gunshots—a frequent finding in research on firearm injuries—but twice as likely to be hospitalized for unintentional gun injuries and more than *eighteen* times as likely to be hospitalized for an intentional gun assault.

The study covered the years from 1998 to 2011, and the good news was that overall, children were less likely to be admitted to a hospital for a gunshot wound at the end of that fourteen-year period than at the beginning. But when the researchers broke down the statistics by race and by the intent behind the shooting, a more complicated and considerably less happy picture emerged. The overall drop in children's hospitalizations for gun injuries was mostly driven by the decline in *unintentional* gunshot wounds, mainly among whites. White and Hispanic children also saw a decline in injuries from intentional gun assaults. But while black children's chances of going to the hospital due to unintentional gunshots fell, too, the number of hospitalizations of black children who had been shot on purpose actually *rose*, albeit modestly, during that fourteen-year period. Indeed, black children who had been intentionally shot were the only group to experience rising rates of hospitalization for gun injuries during that time.[22]

V

Some of the most compelling evidence regarding both the depth and the persistence of the racial violence divide comes from studies charting the flow of victims of violence into individual hospitals and trauma centers across the United States. These studies are often done by the emergency room doctors, who are the closest to this crisis on the ground. And they give us a particularly detailed portrait of who those victims are and where they come from.

In one study, a team of researchers at Vanderbilt University looked at all emergency room admissions at the only Level I hospital trauma center in the Nashville area from 2004 to 2009. They compared the gun injury patients with the overall population of patients admitted to the emergency room for any reason—and, within the gunshot admissions, compared those who had been victims of deliberate assault with those who had been shot accidentally or by their own hand.[23]

Blacks accounted for roughly 30 percent of overall admissions to the emergency room during those years, a proportion generally comparable to their share of the population in Nashville and the surrounding area. But they were three times more likely than "non-black" patients to present with a gunshot wound of any kind. (Note that this study, like some others, collapsed all "non-black" patients, including Hispanics, into one category, which minimizes the gap between black and non-Hispanic white victims.) And the disparity widened considerably for gun injuries resulting from deliberate assault. "Non-black" gun injury patients were most likely to come to the emergency room with accidental or self-inflicted gun wounds: only about 40 percent of them were victims of violent assault. But 66 percent of blacks presenting with gun injuries had been deliberately shot by someone else. Twenty of the patients came to the emergency room with gunshot wounds *more than once* during the years covered by the study; all twenty were black men between the ages of eighteen and thirty.

Another study focusing on a hospital trauma center, this one in Newark, New Jersey, adds more detail to the picture. From 2000 through 2011, more than sixty-three hundred people were treated in this trauma center for injuries sustained in gun assaults: an average of more than five hundred a year, or roughly ten a week. The overwhelming majority—86 percent—were black, and another 9 percent were Hispanic. Half were between twenty and thirty years old, and more than nine out of ten were male. And those proportions—with most victims black, young, and male— changed barely at all during the twelve years covered by the study.[24]

A look at where these young men lived, and where they were shot, reveals an extraordinary concentration of violence in particular places within this generally high-violence region. Almost half the injuries were sustained by people who lived in just 15 percent of the area's census tracts, mostly clustered in especially violent areas within the cities of Newark, Irvington, and East Orange. These census tracts also stood out for their high rates of poverty, low median income, and low educational attainment. And the victims were shot, most often, close to home—more than half of them within a mile, and a fourth within one city block, of where they lived.

The years covered by the study, from 2000 to 2011, were ones in which the national media frequently said that violent crime in the United States was "plummeting." The Newark study shows something very different. The researchers describe a "constant flow" of gun violence victims into the local trauma center throughout these years; indeed, there was "a significant escalation in the extent and severity of gun assault injury observed during this period." Victims presenting with gun assault injuries were more than twice as likely at the end of the period than at the beginning to have suffered three or more wounds, to have been injured in three or more body regions, and to have been shot in especially critical places—the brain or spinal cord. As a consequence, while about 9 percent of these patients died of their injuries in 2000, the figure rose to 14 percent by the end of the study period.

Newark was by no means an isolated case. In Miami-Dade County, Florida (where, in the 1990s, the city had put up road signs cautioning tourists against even driving through the city's most violent neighborhoods), researchers from the University of Miami found that both the total number of patients with violent gun injuries and the number who died of them rose modestly between 2002 and 2012. Despite accounting for only 19 percent of the county's population, blacks were 72 percent of victims coming to the trauma center with firearm assault injuries. They averaged just twenty-seven years of age, eight years younger than white patients with gunshot wounds. As in Newark, the Miami gun violence victims were not only disproportionately black and young but also came overwhelmingly from a relative handful of deeply disadvantaged and highly segregated neighborhoods and were typically shot very close to where they lived. Notably, these locations were virtually unchanged throughout the twelve years of the study: the geographical center of violent assaults in Miami consistently lay somewhere within five contiguous census tracts in the historically volatile areas of Opa-Locka, Overtown, and Liberty City, areas characterized by low income and high levels of unemployment.[25]

Another long-running emergency room study has given us a particularly detailed portrait of the ways in which these extreme levels of community violence play out in the lives of the most vulnerable young people. The city of Flint, Michigan, has become an international symbol of urban abandonment in the United States. Its grim reputation mostly derives from the infamous water crisis that exposed much of its population to high levels of lead and other toxins, subjecting many of the city's children to neurological damage. But the plague of toxic drinking water was only one of a host of intertwined ills in this perennially neglected city. Flint's average household income is just over $26,000 a year; the average owner-occupied housing unit is worth only $28,000, and more than two in five of its residents live below the poverty line.[26] Flint is also routinely ranked among the most violent cities in the United States.

A team of researchers from the University of Michigan has been studying youth violence in Flint for years, focusing on young people entering the busy emergency room at the city's Level I trauma hospital. Between 2009 and 2011, the researchers interviewed a group of over seven hundred Flint youth aged fourteen to twenty-four who went to the emergency room for an assault-related injury and a similarly sized comparison group who were seen in the ER for other reasons.[27] The first thing that stands out about these young people is the sheer amount of serious violence they experienced. More than half of youth seen for an assault injury reported that they'd had a weapon used against them in the past six months; so did a quarter of those who were seen for some other reason. Assault-injured youth were astonishingly likely to have previously gone to the emergency room for one reason or another, averaging 4.6 ER visits just over the course of the past year. Over that time, almost 10 percent of them had been to the emergency room for another assault and 5 percent for a mental health issue. Two-thirds of the assault-injured youth—a group that was, notably, about half female—had experienced partner violence in the past six months.

The encounters that got these youth to the emergency room overwhelmingly involved people they knew, especially acquaintances and romantic partners; only about a quarter involved strangers. The violence took place for a gamut of reasons, some of them very mundane: nearly a quarter of the incidents involved issues of "territory," while another quarter simply involved someone being "angry" or "in a bad mood." Almost 40 percent of the incidents involved either self-defense or retaliation against a previous attack.

The Michigan researchers found, moreover, that violence was not only widespread among Flint's youth but also hard to escape. Those who were victimized once were at very high risk of being victimized again, typically sooner rather than later. Nearly two in five youth who came to the emergency room for a violence-related injury in 2009–2011 suffered another one over the following two years, and 10 percent more than once. Notably, again, almost half of those returning to the hospital after another violent assault were female.[28]

The research also confirmed that in Flint, as in the country as a whole, an extraordinary proportion of the assaults involved firearms. Guns were widely carried by Flint's youth: about one in four reported carrying a gun in the six months before their initial admission to the emergency room. (Since some youth may not have wanted to admit carrying one, this is probably an underestimate of the real number.) Over the two years after admission, an astonishing 22 percent of the entire group were victimized in a firearm conflict, some more than once. In total, the roughly six hundred youths in this sample collectively reported 183 incidents during that two-year period in which they were "threatened or shot at by someone else with a firearm."[29]

In another study, the Michigan researchers found that sexual violence, too, was remarkably prevalent among the Flint youth, both male and female. They defined sexual violence narrowly, including only forcible or nonconsensual intercourse—but even by this strict definition, 22 percent of their sample reported having been victimized during their lifetimes when they were first interviewed. (And that figure actually understates the extent of sexual violence among youth entering the Flint emergency room, since the researchers opted to exclude those who came to the hospital *because of* sexual assault from their sample.) Almost one in eight experienced at least one episode of sexual violence during the two-year follow-up period, with black youth nearly twice as likely to be victimized over this time as non-black youth. And as with violence more generally, sexual violence was hard to escape: those who had suffered a sexual assault in the past were almost three times as likely to suffer another in the two years after their initial emergency room visit.[30]

The Michigan researchers concluded that "violence is pervasive among youth living in this community."[31] And the concentration of violence in places like Flint is indeed extreme. But it's also important to understand that the racial divide in American violence is such that even living in a much better-off community is no guarantee of personal security for African Americans.

In a recent study of firearm assaults in Philadelphia in 2013–14, the researchers found a depressingly familiar pattern: black Philadelphians were shot at five times the rate of white Philadelphians, and gun violence was overwhelmingly concentrated among young black men. Both blacks and whites were more likely to be shot in the city's poorer neighborhoods. Strikingly, however, the racial disparity steadily *increased* along with rising neighborhood income. In the poorest neighborhoods, with a median household income below $20,000, blacks were shot at a rate roughly one and a half times that of whites. In more affluent communities, rates of gun violence were lower for both whites and blacks. But while they "decreased to near zero" for whites as neighborhood income rose, they declined much less dramatically for blacks. The result was that in communities with average household incomes over $60,000, blacks faced a nearly *sixteenfold* greater chance of being shot than whites. In fact, blacks living in those high-income areas were more likely to be shot than whites who lived in neighborhoods with average incomes of only $20,000 to $30,000 a year.[32]

Researchers can and do argue about the specifics. But the overall picture is stunningly consistent. In a country that suffers far more intentional violence than any other advanced industrial nation, African Americans suffer it all out of proportion to their share of the population. That is true whether the violence is fatal or nonfatal, committed with guns or knives or fists, committed in the home or on the street. It is true for young and old, men and women, middle-class and poor. These racial differences are not subtle: they are glaring, and they are numbingly predictable. And they are not going away.

The impact of endemic violence, moreover, does not end with the damage done to the lives and bodies of individual victims. As we'll see in the next chapter, concentrated violence stamps virtually every aspect of life in the places most affected by it: the mental and physical health of community residents, the way parents raise their children, the way young people envision their futures, and much more.

TWO

IMPACTS

In the late 1980s, the psychiatrist Carl Bell and the psychologist Esther Jenkins asked over five hundred African American schoolchildren on Chicago's South Side about violent incidents they had witnessed. Of these second to eighth graders, more than one in four said they had seen a shooting; nearly 30 percent said they had seen someone stabbed. In a later sample of more than a thousand students from middle and high schools in the same area, the numbers rose even higher: 39 percent had witnessed a shooting, 35 percent had witnessed a stabbing, and close to one in four said they had "seen someone get killed." In nearly half of these incidents, students had known the victims: they were family members, friends, neighbors, or classmates.[1]

As Bell and Jenkins pointed out, these numbers were

based on children's self-reports, and there is a possibility that they may have sometimes been exaggerating for effect. But a very similar picture emerged when parents in high-violence neighborhoods were asked about their children's experience of violence. Interviewing mothers in a Chicago housing project around the same time, the developmental psychologist James Garbarino and his colleagues found that nearly all said their children had been exposed to a shooting by age five and "identified 'shooting' as their main safety concern for their children."[2]

Bell and Jenkins noted two characteristics of this pervasive violence that amplified its potential impact on the community and, in particular, on its children: it was often "random" and "public," and it was "chronic." Though violence usually took place among people who knew each other, and often indoors, they noted that a "distressing amount of unpredictable, life-threatening violence occurs in public places, exposing innocent bystanders" and turning some hard-hit communities into "veritable war zones."[3] Garbarino and his colleagues made the same observation: the "chronic" danger that suffused the most violent neighborhoods was very different from "acute" danger. It is bad enough if a "deranged individual enters a normally safe school and opens fire with a rifle," they noted. But chronic, ongoing danger—as in "war, communal violence, or chronic violent crime"—is likely to cause even more profound psychological effects. Like Bell and Jenkins, Garbarino and his colleagues used the term "war zone" to describe the hardest-hit communities, and it was not an idle comparison. "What children experience in parts of

Southside Chicago," they wrote, "was strikingly and fatefully similar to what children experienced in Cambodia during the Pol Pot regime, Northern Ireland during the Catholic/Protestant 'troubles,' or Gaza under Israeli occupation."[4]

I

Three decades after these observations, the picture is disturbingly similar. In many—though by no means all—of the affected communities, the level of life-threatening violence has gone down somewhat since the time when these studies were done, during one of deadliest periods in recent American history. But the presence of chronic violence still suffuses the lives of children and parents.

A recent survey by researchers at Yale's School of Public Health, for example, found that exposure to violence was "pervasive" in six low-income neighborhoods in New Haven.[5] Almost three out of every four residents had heard gunshots in their neighborhood; 40 percent said they heard them at least once a month. Exposure to violence was frequent among all residents of these highly disadvantaged communities, of whatever race or ethnicity, but it was much worse for blacks: 80 percent of black residents, versus 57 percent of whites, had heard gunshots in their neighborhood "more than once." One in three blacks, versus 18 percent of whites, had a family member or close friend who had been "hurt by violent act in neighborhood"; fully one in four had a family member or close friend *killed* by such an act. Young black men in particular, ages eighteen to thirty-four, were almost six times as likely as young white men—even within these poor and consistently troubled communities—to have had a family member or friend killed this way.[6]

Similarly, in interviews with more than six hundred young African Americans, half male and half female, enrolled in a job training center in Baltimore, researchers from Johns Hopkins University found that more than half of them reported having been exposed to violence in their neighborhood. The study's subjects, aged sixteen to thirty-three, were drawn from especially poor communities within a city generally characterized by both deep poverty and endemic violence. The researchers defined "neighborhood violence" in fairly extreme terms: this was beyond ordinary fights in the schoolyard. The survey asked four questions: "Have you seen someone beaten, shot, or really hurt by someone?"; "Have you ever had to hide because of shootings in your neighborhood?"; "Have you ever been around people shooting guns?"; and "Have you ever witnessed a homicide?" Three out of five young men, and two out of five young women, reported being exposed to this level of neighborhood violence just within the past year.[7]

It's important to be clear about what these studies do not say. They do not say that *everyone* living in a high-violence neighborhood is routinely victimized by violence. If we look back at the New Haven study, for example, while it is true that nearly a third of black residents of high-risk neighborhoods had a family member or friend who had been hurt by violence, the flip side is that two-thirds did not.

Likewise, fully one-third of people living in New Haven's high-risk neighborhoods said they were afraid that they or someone close to them would be the victim of violence in the future, but this also means that two-thirds did not.[8] Even within generally high-violence neighborhoods, the risk is most concentrated among particular residents, often within fairly tight networks of people engaged in especially risky behavior themselves. It is important not to exaggerate what are already troubling enough figures.

But it is also crucial not to minimize them. What these figures tell us is that serious violence is an astonishingly common part of the lived experience of low-income African Americans in the United States and that this experience—as a witness or as a victim—starts very early. And what is especially troubling is its persistence: the tragic continuity between the observations of Bell and Jenkins in the late 1980s, or James Garbarino's from around the same time, and the present. That one in four black residents of New Haven's poorest neighborhoods say they have suffered the death of a family member or friend from neighborhood violence is bad enough; that they say this more than two decades after the start of the much-celebrated "crime drop" in America is particularly sobering.

II

The pervasive presence of violence means that people who live in especially dangerous communities must develop strategies to avoid it. There is a growing body of research on the ways in which people manage their daily lives, and their children's lives, in order to "navigate" communities where violence is common. Those strategies are often at least partly successful; indeed, the fact that they have become routine in places where violence is socially and geographically concentrated helps explain why the statistics about victimization are not even higher than they are. But they also come with substantial costs.

As far back as the late 1980s, James Garbarino and his colleagues described the variety of restrictions that mothers in Chicago public housing imposed on their children to protect them from what the mothers perceived as nearly overwhelming dangers. They prohibited their children from playing outside, "for fear of shooting incidents," and adopted a "very restrictive and punitive style of discipline (including physical assault) in an effort to prevent the child from falling under the influence of negative forces" in the community. These strategies were likely to cause problems of their own—hindering the children's ability to engage in ordinary and healthy pursuits and, in the case of excessive physical discipline, potentially fueling aggression that could get them in trouble later in life. But the researchers argued that the mothers' choices were not surprising: they were often caught in a bind, forced to "choose between the lesser of two evils."[9]

Twenty-five years later, interviewing black single mothers of nine- to thirteen-year-old daughters in a low-income housing project in Newark, New Jersey, Janice Johnson

Dias and Robert Whitaker found that parents still faced that choice. Faced with the responsibility of raising daughters in an environment they saw as overwhelmingly threatening, a startling 94 percent of mothers said that they "did not let their daughters participate in any outdoor play in their neighborhood" during the school year. "You actually have a neighborhood held hostage," a mother told Dias and Whitaker.[10] What made the neighborhood's violence so daunting, for these women, was that it was both literally close to home and unnervingly unpredictable—a threat that began just outside their door, if not inside it. "A girl got shot on 22nd St. just sitting on her porch," another mother noted. "Bullets go flying. A little baby got shot. I don't do the porch thing that much."

"I'm scared of her to go outside, because I don't know what's going to happen to her when she hits outside," a third mother explained:

> Which is as far as a car coming up on the sidewalk or somebody randomly shooting off a gun, or just these young kids nowadays just want to beat up on people because they're pretty or they have a long hair or because they have a short hair or because they look a certain way or dress differently. I just don't agree with her going outside at this day and age because it's too much crazy stuff in this world now. It's too much.

For the women Dias and Whitaker spoke with, violence was not manageably confined to just some places and people in the neighborhood. They taught their daughters some important "dos and don'ts," as one put it, including particular areas and situations to avoid. But they didn't believe that these tactics would necessarily be enough to protect them:

> A lot of times by her knowing all of these things it wouldn't have anything to do with her getting hurt out there one day. Just by being out where she's standing at for some apparent reason something happened. And she gets messed up in a crossfire or something. Bad things happen to good people that have nothing to do with it and innocent people, you see what I'm saying. . . . And that's what I'm very scared of.

As one of the women put it, "I just wouldn't want to one day come home, or come outside, and it's my daughter laying on the sidewalk because she done got hit by a 12-year-old boy that was driving a stolen car. So to avoid all that I just wouldn't let her outside." To play outside at all, the girls had to leave the immediate neighborhood— for instance, by going to a relative's house. As the researchers put it, "safe play means leaving home."[11]

Another decade later, Dexter Voisin of the University of Chicago and his colleagues found similar strategies among parents of adolescents from highly segregated communities on Chicago's South Side.[12] Though the parents—fathers and mothers—who participated in these Chicago focus groups were a generally less deprived group than the mothers in Dias and Whitaker's Newark study, they, too, saw their community as an inescapably dangerous place—not just for their children, but for everyone. A common theme was that there were "no safe havens": that "few if any places within the community could be considered safe from violence," including churches, schools, and public transportation. Parents spoke of gun violence taking place "against preachers in the pulpit and during funeral services, or of people being robbed while at church." "There was a pervasive sense," the researchers wrote,

> that long-held community traditions of respecting the older individuals and the sacred were being torn down and debased by widespread community violence . . . [and that] there was an increasing universal vulnerability to community violence irrespective of age, gender, or clerical status and that such acts were random, senseless, and could occur anywhere or to anyone.

The sense that community violence had burst through these traditional boundaries was a recurrent theme among the parents. "People are shooting in churches," one of the interviewees said. "Imagine on church doors they have stickers saying 'no guns allowed' . . . crazy you have to put that on church doors." Another recalled how "this mother was sitting on the porch holding her baby and someone passed by and started shooting up the house and the baby took several bullets and died. . . . An innocent baby murdered who has not done nothing to anyone and not even gotten a chance to live or even learn to walk."

The parents also noted the threat of violence by police as an important element in the generally threatening neighborhood environment—and an especially consequential one, since it meant that neither children nor parents could rely on police to protect them from the communal violence that surrounded them. Asking police for help could actually be an invitation to further harm.

Faced with violence that was ubiquitous and unpredictable, the Chicago parents, like the mothers in Newark, adopted a range of strategies to steer children away from it as best they could. The researchers categorized these as "sheltering, chauffeuring, and removal." Sheltering meant insisting that children avoid especially dangerous places and sharply restricting their activities, confining their days almost entirely to school and home. Sheltering, in turn, often required chauffeuring: "I don't let my kids get on the bus or walk down the street." "If I don't have enough gas that day—and I'm going to be honest with you—to take them to school, they not going." "Removal" often meant sending their kids to schools outside the neighborhood, since the local ones were widely regarded as unsafe spaces. But all of these defensive strategies had their drawbacks. Sheltering children from the neighborhood, or sending them to distant schools, meant that they were deprived of local friends—who, among other things, could provide some protection against community violence. And parents often

felt that these strategies hindered their children's "matura-
tion": "You'll end up with eighteen-, twenty-one-year-olds
who've never been on a bus."

The anxieties expressed by parents in such communities are shared by their children. In New Haven, black and
Hispanic students from low-income neighborhoods told
Yale researchers that they saw their surroundings as dangerous.[13] "It's crazy," said an eighth-grade girl. "You're in
the hood and like . . . you go out and you die." Another
eighth grader concurred: "I'm afraid if I go outside that
something might happen to me. . . . I'm not supposed to
feel like that. . . . I shouldn't be afraid to walk outside."

Some of the New Haven children regarded violence
as an essentially uncontrollable fact of life. "You see . . .
violence every day," one said. "You can't stop it; you can't do
anything about it." In order to avoid it, they often sharply
restricted their activities. A fifth grader summed up his cir-
cumscribed routine: "You stay at home, read your books,
go to school, go back home, play safely, do the same thing
all over again." Another student told the researchers, "No
one open the door after 8 o'clock."

Black children in West Philadelphia, ages ten to sixteen, interviewed by researchers from the University of
Pennsylvania, likewise developed "constant vigilance and
exquisite sensitivity" to neighborhood violence—what
the researchers called a "finely tuned system of assessing
their neighborhoods that was constantly 'on.'"[14] "A little boy got shot around the corner," one girl said. "I just
go you know, to the corner store sometimes, but that's

only right there at the corner of my block. So, I don't feel unsafe."

"Navigating the neighborhood took a constant, conscious effort," the researchers wrote. "Youth were clear about settings that they knew were unsafe and had strategies to avoid those settings."[15] As one of the children explained:

> I know my way around the neighborhood and I know what type of people live around there and who lives where and all that kind of stuff. . . . There's not too many places I go by myself except over to the park, and I feel pretty safe there cause most of my friends be over there.[16]

Not surprisingly, youth who are better able to "navigate" their environment in these ways are more likely to escape the violence that surrounds them. But the focus on what some researchers call "street efficacy" can be taken too far, to the point of suggesting that teaching people to "read" the fraught terrain of violent communities can substitute for addressing the conditions that make that kind of navigation necessary in the first place.[17] Some observers come uncomfortably close to blaming community residents for their own victimization. In this view, people living in even the most violent communities can stay clear of trouble if they want to—all they need to do is learn the techniques of successful navigation of dangerous territory. It's true that people who hang out with gang members or sell drugs on the street do indeed put themselves at great risk.

But this perspective sidesteps two crucial realities. First, as the studies from Newark, Chicago, and West Philadelphia clearly show, in the most dangerous communities violence can strike anyone, often unpredictably. Second, and even more important, this attitude prompts the question of why some people in some communities in America—and not others—should have to learn to "navigate" their streets in this way, just to have a reasonable chance of achieving a level of elementary safety that others can take for granted.

III

"Exposure to violence," the terminology often used by researchers, is in fact a vague and rather antiseptic way to describe the experience of violence in the communities that suffer it the most. "Exposure" can mean hearing about a shooting a few blocks away; it can also mean losing a friend, a child, a sibling, or a parent to homicide. And one of the most devastating impacts of the racial disparity in violent death in America is that it creates what Jocelyn Smith of the University of Maryland calls "unequal burdens of loss."[18]

Smith interviewed forty young men, ages eighteen to twenty-four, who were clients of a youth program in an East Baltimore neighborhood where nearly nine in ten residents were black and just under half of the families lived below the poverty line. She sought to explore how often they had to deal with "traumatic loss" and how it affected them. Between them, the forty young men—who, again, were all under twenty-five at the time of the interviews—had collectively experienced 267 deaths of "peers, biological family members, and other important adults in their lives." Nearly half—45 percent—of those deaths were homicides. Only three of the forty youths had *not* suffered the loss of someone close to them from homicide. The other thirty-seven had suffered an average of three homicide losses each, ranging from only one to as many as ten. Thirteen had experienced their first loss by age twelve (the youngest at age four), and all but nine of them before they turned eighteen. Eight out of the forty had "experienced multiple homicide deaths in a single year during adolescence."

The impact of those losses, Smith found, was wide-ranging and profound, even in the short term. The frequent deaths of people close to them "crystallized the lethality of neighborhood violence and created a sense of personal vulnerability to violent death among participants." One youth spoke of how he now had to "watch for stuff I'm not even suppose to be watching out for like stray bullets and all types of stuff when no child should be worrying about stuff like that, you know? Shouldn't nobody be worried about that."

Pervasive losses, Smith wrote, also "disrupted young men's social relationships and altered the structure of their social networks"—a somewhat elaborate way of saying that they lost the people they used to hang out with. "I'm losing friends because my friends is getting killed—some of my close friends," an eighteen-year-old lamented. "And then, it just, like, be nothing else left. If I got no friends then like what I'm supposed to do? I just sit in the house now. It's no friends that I have." The frequency of their losses, Smith concluded, "cognitively and emotionally exhausted" these young homicide survivors, creating "contexts of protracted vulnerability in which black males had to negotiate constant threats to their own mortality while processing the deaths of their peers."[19]

There are other losses, too, for young people living in communities hard hit by endemic violence. They not only lose people close to them; they also often lose faith in a secure future—or any future. Bell and Jenkins wrote about this sense of "futurelessness" a generation ago,[20] and research since then has confirmed their insight. As one nineteen-year-old Atlanta youth told researchers from Georgia State University: "I grew up with shooting and fighting all over. You grew up with books and shit. Where I come from you never know if you going to live one minute to the next. . . . People die every day."[21]

Tellingly, when the researchers asked these Atlanta youth to quantify their chances of being killed in the next five years—50 percent? more? less?—almost all "struggled to answer." This was not because they didn't understand the question but because it "seemed pointless to concern themselves with the 'distant' future, especially when their more immediate survival was not something that could be taken for granted." The fact that five years counted as a "distant" future for these young men is itself illuminating. As one of them put it:

> Shit man, I don't know. . . . Flip a coin. I say an equal chance, a good chance, I could be dead. But there's no point to it, to talk about it. I got to keep on doing what I be doing and just see how long it goes. Ain't no point to giving you a number. The number don't mean nothing. Cuz I got to live another day or I could live forever, you know what I'm saying.[22]

The researchers found that this sense of the ever-present possibility of early death didn't seem to inspire fear among these young men; instead, "the prospect of an untimely death was accepted as a fact of life." Echoing the work of Garbarino and his colleagues a generation before, they noted that black youths' attitudes toward death in Atlanta "seem to resemble the coping responses that develop among individuals in war-torn countries."[23]

As this suggests, under conditions of extreme danger such "discounting" of the future may be a useful, "adaptive" response. It prepares the youths for the loss of people they care about and stiffens their resolve to go on with life—to continue "doin' what I'm doin.'" But it can also backfire in the long run by undercutting the capacity to commit to endeavors that call for long-term planning and focus, like schooling and work. What sense is there in carefully preparing for the future if you're not certain that there will be one? As we will see in more detail later, the sense of futurelessness often breeds a kind of nihilism: if dying early is a strong possibility, getting what you can in the here and now is all that makes sense or really matters. And in a vicious circle, that state of mind helps to perpetuate the pervasive communal violence that imperils futures in the first place.

IV

The pioneering observers of the impact of endemic violence were especially concerned with its potential consequences for mental health, particularly in children. Carl Bell and Esther Jenkins argued in 1991 that exposure to chronic violence created a range of "pernicious effects" on children's mental health that were often subtle and, as a result, often underestimated. Children's "immersion in a violent milieu" could, for example, lead to symptoms of post-traumatic stress disorder, even if they had not been directly victimized. Bell and Jenkins cited research showing that children exposed to pervasive community violence often reexperienced the events "in play, dreams, or intrusive images and sounds"; they also suffered from "psychic numbing," leading to inactivity and "constricted affect." They were often afraid that the violence would happen again and became pessimistic about the future. They had trouble forming interpersonal relationships, in part because the belief that they would "not reach adulthood" made them "hesitate to establish bonds that they fear will be broken."[24] James Garbarino and his colleagues similarly argued, on the basis of their observations of "war zones" from Cambodia to Chicago, that exposure to chronic danger "imposes a requirement for developmental adjustment—accommodations that are likely to include persistent PTSD, alterations of personality, and major changes in patterns of behavior."[25]

A great deal of sophisticated research over the last three decades both affirms and complicates this picture. It shows that though many people who live in violence-torn communities are subjected to the kind of danger that can lead to psychological trauma, that outcome isn't written in stone—partly because, rather than being simply passive victims of that threatening environment, they often adapt to it in ways that help to make it more tolerable emotionally. Still, there is no question that living with pervasive violence often shapes young lives and minds in ways that can be deeply harmful. The harm is not necessarily indelible, but it is difficult to escape it altogether. And, again, some of the strategies designed to avoid it may serve to perpetuate the violence that made them necessary in the first place.

Understanding exactly how living in an environment of constant threats of violence affects personality and behavior is complicated—particularly because it's difficult to tease out the specific effects of witnessing violence (or being its victim) from other aspects of the environment that might affect mental health. We know, for example, that growing up in poverty greatly increases the risks of many kinds of mental illness. So if children in a poor neighborhood who witness a great deal of violence end up with unusually high levels of, say, depression, it isn't easy to determine whether the depression was caused by their exposure to violence or simply their poverty.

But an abundance of research now confirms that living in a chronically violent community makes a difference: it raises the risks of adverse consequences for mental health over and above the effects of poverty, even for many children who are not directly victimized. That doesn't mean that all children are affected in the same ways or to the same degree. It's always a mistake to assume that people's experiences are all alike, even in the context of broadly similar social conditions—or to regard them just as reactive victims of those circumstances. But it is increasingly clear that being surrounded by violence takes a profound emotional toll, in one way or another.

Much of the early research on the subject was informed by what has been called a "traumatic stress" model, which suggests a linear relationship between violence and damage to children's mental health: the more violence the children have been exposed to, the greater their chances of developing depression, withdrawal, and anxiety. Some of the recent research supports this model. The study by Johns Hopkins University researchers of young African Americans at a job training center in Baltimore, for example, found a clear and direct link between violence and depression in the more than six hundred youth in their sample. The connection held for several kinds of violence exposure: witnessing community violence, experiencing violence in a partner relationship, or being forced to have sex. Youths who had been exposed to serious neighborhood violence were more than twice as likely to report suffering from depressive symptoms as those who had not; those who had experienced forced sex, two and a half times as likely. These lines crossed gender categories, and they grew stronger as the number of exposures increased. Thus, youths who had been exposed to community violence *and* forced to have sex were seven times as likely to suffer depressive symptoms as those with no exposure to violence: those exposed to partner violence as well, eight times as likely. The effect was "additive": the more violence, and the more kinds of violence, these young people experienced, the more likely they were to be depressed.[26]

That outcome makes sense intuitively, but other research paints a more complex picture. In a study of over four hundred inner-city minority sixth graders, for example, Daisy Ng-Mak of Columbia University and her colleagues explored the ways in which violence exposure related to both aggressive behavior (such as "carrying a hidden weapon" or "using a weapon to get money from others") and what psychologists call "internalizing" disorders, including depression and anxiety.[27] They found that the relationship between exposure to violence and aggression was indeed additive—that is, the more the children were exposed to violence, the more aggressive they became. But when it came to psychological distress, things were more complicated. At lower to moderate levels of violence exposure, children did seem to become more depressed as their exposure increased. But beyond a certain point, exposure to violence no longer had the same effect. Contrary to the earlier research, once the level of violence got high enough, children began to be *less* distressed, not more.

The children who had experienced very high levels of violence were a relatively small proportion of their sixth-grade sample. But they constituted a particularly troubling group. "A minority of youngsters," Ng-Mak and her colleagues wrote, "exhibited excessive aggression but reduced symptoms of psychological distress in the context of high levels of community violence exposure. These children, highly aggressive and not deterred by feelings of distress, may be most at risk for violent delinquent behavior as they proceed through adolescence."[28] The researchers suggested that this group, instead of being traumatized by the experience of extreme violence, responded to it with an "emotional numbing or cognitive desensitization."

Other studies support that conclusion. Sylvie Mrug and her colleagues, for example, found a similar pattern in a sample of over seven hundred children, three-quarters of them African American, in and around Birmingham, Alabama. The children were recruited into the study in fifth grade and followed up until age eighteen. The researchers considered violence exposure in three different contexts: the community, the school, and the home. As in other studies, these children were exposed to a great deal of violence. Anywhere from 77 percent to 86 percent of them, depending on the age at which they were interviewed, had experienced violence in at least one of the three settings; more than a third had experienced violence in more than one setting by age eleven.[29]

As in Ng-Mak's Columbia study, "internalizing" psychological symptoms among these Alabama children showed what Mrug and her colleagues described as an "inverted U" pattern: that is, children's psychological distress rose along with greater exposure to violence up to a point but then began to fall, such that those who were *most* exposed were no more affected internally than those who rarely experienced violence at all. Children who fell in the middle range—who experienced moderate levels of violence—did suffer high levels of distress, and that seemed to inhibit them from becoming violent themselves as they grew older. But for children whose exposure to violence passed beyond a certain line, distress (and its presumably inhibiting effects) *diminished*, and their tendency to engage in violence of their own increased.

The Alabama researchers, like Ng-Mak's group, estimated that only a relatively small proportion—about 10 percent—of the children in their study fit that troubling category. But they amounted to "a sizable minority of urban youth who may be experiencing emotional desensitization to real-life violence," and who accordingly "are at the greatest risk for serious violence in the future." These effects were especially pronounced for children who had been exposed to violence in multiple contexts, for whom violence came to seem "ubiquitous and inescapable."[30]

The psychological impact of growing up surrounded by chronic violence, then, is complex, and it depends on many factors: the level and type of exposure, how long it lasts, whether there are sources of support and assistance available to buffer the impact, and more.[31] But the bottom line is that, as James Garbarino and his colleagues put it a generation ago, few young people escape these surroundings completely "unscathed" emotionally.[32] Some may suffer from depression, anxiety, or post-traumatic stress disorder; others might avoid "internalizing" the impact of violence in their lives, but at the expense of shutting down emotionally and, at the extreme, becoming aggressive in their own right.

This is not to deny the extraordinary resilience shown by many children who grow up in even the most volatile circumstances. Nothing in this body of research suggests that the psychological impacts of endemic violence are uniform, or necessarily crippling or permanent.[33] But it does confirm the hard truth that for many children, growing up in these places is a qualitatively different experience: many things that children in other communities generally take for granted cannot be taken for granted here.

V

That endemic violence can have profound impacts on mental health may not be surprising. But we now also increasingly understand that living with chronic violence can influence physical health, too. In a very real sense, endemic violence literally "gets into the body"—affecting everything from cardiovascular and respiratory health to the functioning of the immune system and the quality of sleep.[34]

As with mental health, teasing out the specific contribution of violence from all the other ways in which poverty plays havoc with the body isn't easy. But the best studies make it clear that though chronic violence is not the only factor, nor an isolated one, it can be independently harmful—and in an astonishing variety of ways. Children who report having heard gunshots in their community more than once and being afraid to leave home because of the threat of violence, for example, are more than three times as likely to develop asthma as their peers who have experienced neither of those things.[35] Chronic exposure to community violence appears to affect the "HPA axis," the system that regulates responses to stress. Specifically, chronic violence may interfere with the regulation of cortisol, the hormone that controls the so-called fight-or-flight response, in ways that affect levels of hyperactivity and aggression.[36] It can also exacerbate immune system problems. Among youth with preexisting HIV, for example, those who experience high levels of community violence have a higher "viral load"—indicating that their body has a weakened ability to fight the HIV infection.[37] One of the strongest findings connects chronic violence exposure to cardiovascular problems, especially high blood pressure.[38] More generally, some research finds a small but significant link between increases in community violence and several "stress-responsive" disorders, including fatal heart attacks, anxiety, and substance use.[39] And living in violent neighborhoods has been linked to excessive weight gain and other problems during pregnancy.[40]

One of the most telling impacts of chronic violence involves sleep.[41] We may not immediately think of sleep as something that is powerfully shaped by social conditions. But as one recent study notes, sleep "does not occur in a vacuum."[42] How well we sleep depends on where we live and where we stand on the social and economic ladder, and a growing body of research highlights the particularly corrosive impact of "sleep disparities" between the poor—especially the minority poor—and everyone else. And those disparities have consequences. Poor sleep has been implicated in a host of "somatic, psychological and behavioral problems" among adolescents, including aggression, self-harm, and impulsivity.[43]

The connection between chronic violence and sleep disturbance is compellingly explored in research carried out in Mobile, Alabama—part of a long-term investigation, conducted between 1998 and 2011, of children's lives in a deeply impoverished African American community. If any social environment was likely to undermine children's sleep, this one surely fit the bill. Roughly nine in ten of the children enrolled in the Mobile study were poor enough to be eligible for free school lunches, and violence was an inescapable part of their communities during the years the study took place. More than one in four children said they had "seen someone being cut, stabbed, or shot" during the past three months. Those reporting the most exposure were more likely to suffer from sleep problems, including insomnia, daytime sleepiness, and nightmares. The differences in sleep patterns between them and other children in this community were not huge, since all of them were growing up in similarly volatile and impoverished circumstances. But they were significant—suggesting that beyond the negative impact of poverty, witnessing severe violence had an independent effect of its own.

Unexpectedly, this effect seemed to diminish, especially for boys, as the children aged into their teen years. But the researchers argue that this was not necessarily a positive development. More likely, it reflected the process of "desensitization" we've seen before. As children in this deeply impoverished and routinely dangerous community got older, their response to many kinds of external stress—including being surrounded by violence—became "blunted": they lost less sleep over it simply because they got more used to it.[44]

VI

In the 1980s, Carl Bell and Esther Jenkins observed that children exposed to chronic violence may "show a decline in cognitive performance and school achievement." They believed that this might happen for a variety of reasons: the children might be distracted by "the intrusion of thoughts related to the trauma, making it impossible to concentrate on school material"; they might develop a "cognitive style" of deliberately forgetting troubling memories, which would be counterproductive in school; or they might experience "simple fatigue from sleepless nights." These effects of violence were often overlooked, Bell and Jenkins believed, in part because it was hard to disentangle them from the array of other "destabilizing" factors in their lives that could help explain school problems. But ignoring them would be a serious mistake.[45] And some highly sophisticated research since then confirms and expands their observations.

In a study of public school children in Chicago, for example, the sociologist Patrick Sharkey investigated the effect of local homicides on the performance of children aged five to seventeen on two commonly used tests of reading ability and vocabulary. There were, unfortunately, plenty of homicides to work with—more than six thousand in Chicago during the years of this study, 1994 to 2002—which meant that large numbers of children happened to be assessed on reading and vocabulary shortly after a homicide had taken place close to their home. Indeed, for African American children, one in every eight of these routine assessments happened within four weeks of a homicide in their census tract—another illuminating piece of evidence of the extraordinary suffusion of the city's African American communities during those years by violent death. (Sharkey noted that "exposure to local homicide is much less common among Hispanics and is extremely rare among whites.")[46]

Sharkey found that a homicide occurring in their block group within a week of the vocabulary test reduced African American children's scores significantly. Homicides occurring in their block group within four days of the reading test similarly reduced their scores. Sharkey's findings by themselves can't prove that these effects on test scores have long-term consequences, but he argues that their overwhelming concentration in some neighborhoods and not others may well "have implications for understanding long-range inequality." In a particularly chilling calculation, Sharkey estimates that African American youth living in Chicago's most violent neighborhoods "spend at least one quarter of the year, or roughly one week out of every month, functioning at a low level because of local homicides."[47] Equally startling is that these effects did not depend on the children actually *witnessing* the violence: the sheer occurrence of a killing in their immediate neighborhood was enough to cause them to lose focus and concentration to a degree that showed up in their test performance.

Sharkey's concern about the long-term effects of violence is supported by another Chicago study, by Julia Burdick-Will of Johns Hopkins University, which looked at the effects of growing up in a violent neighborhood on children's standardized test scores over several years—rather than, as in Sharkey's study, observing the "acute" impact within a short time frame. The children in Burdick-Will's study—about thirty-one thousand in all, roughly 90 percent of color—were all enrolled in third grade in Chicago's public schools in the fall of 2002. They were followed until spring 2011, when they should have been in eleventh grade. Burdick-Will measured their initial exposure to violence using police data on the total number of violent crimes that took place in their local block group from the end of second grade to the end of third grade. Thus, as in Sharkey's study, the children merely had to have lived near sites of violent crimes, not necessarily to have witnessed them.

Burdick-Will concluded that "students exposed to violent neighborhoods during childhood fall further behind their peers from safer neighborhoods as they progress through school."[48] Importantly, this was true above and beyond any general effect that living in a *disadvantaged* neighborhood had on performance. Children across poor neighborhoods had roughly similar test scores in third grade, whether or not their community was especially violent. But as the school years went on, those from the more violent neighborhoods progressed more slowly. Since their neighborhoods were otherwise basically similar, Burdick-Will argued, there is "something about the violence alone that influences achievement growth."[49] And the effects of violence are "long-lasting, accumulated over time, and will have implications for learning gaps for many years to come."[50]

These studies all focus on Chicago, a city with no shortage of extremely violent neighborhoods and a highly segregated public school system. But national-level research by David Harding of the University of Michigan shows that Chicago is hardly unique. Harding looked at how the experience of neighborhood violence affects rates of teen pregnancy and high school graduation, using data from a well-known national survey of adolescent health that sampled about 150 schools across the country. He measured neighborhood violence by considering the number of youth who said they had experienced one of several kinds of violence—witnessing a shooting or stabbing, being threatened with a weapon, being shot or stabbed themselves, being "jumped," and being injured in a fight—along with their subjective views on whether the neighborhood was safe and the "chances that one would be killed" there, plus their parents' impression of whether the neighborhood "had a problem with drugs."[51]

As expected, the data showed that adolescents from more disadvantaged neighborhoods were less likely to graduate from high school. But Harding found that high exposure to violence explained a surprisingly large part of that association: about half for young men and fully 90 percent for young women. Community violence, moreover, had similar, though smaller, effects on teen pregnancy. As with school failure, we've known for a long time that teen pregnancy rates are higher in some poor communities. But Harding's study suggests that a significant part of that connection is due specifically to the effects of neighborhood violence. Since both of these outcomes (failing to graduate from high school and getting pregnant as an unmarried teenager) are enormously fateful for young people's later lives, Harding concluded that neighborhood violence—independently of other unfavorable social conditions—"plays a role in the intergenerational trans-mission of economic and social disadvantage."[52]

These findings remind us, once again, of how wide-ranging and insidious the effects of endemic violence can be. And they drive home the reality that violence is not an isolated problem but part of a deeply entwined set of adverse circumstances that tend to reinforce each other. Violence flourishes in conditions of extreme social disadvantage, and it affects people in a myriad of ways—some of which help to perpetuate those very conditions and thus make it likely that violence will remain concentrated precisely where it has always been concentrated, in spite of the most drastic efforts at suppression and containment. It is time, then, to explore those deeper social conditions in more detail.

THREE

EXPLANATIONS, I: PIONEERS

Efforts to explain the high levels of violence in many black communities stretch back well over a hundred years. The earliest studies of race and violence lacked the sophisticated research techniques available to more modern scholars, and the older writing can sound a little quaint to modern ears. Critics have argued that some of this work is laced with the racial and class stereotypes of its time, and often obscures the full humanity of black Americans and the strengths that lie within their communities. But much of what these scholars had to say about the links between racial inequality and violence remains revealing and compelling. They illuminated the mechanisms by which structural oppression translates into personal and communal harm, providing crucial insights that are still important in helping to unravel the causes of violent death and injury in black communities—and that, as we'll see in chapter 4, are generally supported by more recent research. So the work of these pioneers commands our attention.

I

In the summer of 1896, a young W.E.B. Du Bois went to Philadelphia at the invitation of the University of Pennsylvania to conduct a study of "Negro" life in the city, moving with his family into a room over a cafeteria in "the worst part of the Seventh Ward." He had no romantic illusions about his new quarters. "We lived," he later recalled, "in the midst of an atmosphere of dirt, drunkenness, poverty and crime. Murder sat on our doorsteps, police were our government, and philanthropy dropped in with periodic advice."[1]

Du Bois spent the next year and a half producing one of the most compelling pieces of social research of his time— published, just as the twentieth century was about to begin, as *The Philadelphia Negro: A Social Study*. With only limited assistance from a few students, Du Bois created an extraordinarily detailed picture of black life in a major northern city at the close of the nineteenth century. He examined demographics, family life, education, work, health, housing, and politics. He looked into Negro religion and organized social life, at poverty, at their relations with whites—and, not least, at crime. It is a work of astonishing breadth and still stands as a landmark in American social science.

To be sure, reading *The Philadelphia Negro* from the perspective of twenty-first-century sensibilities can be jarring. Du Bois had very strong views about social class—what his biographer describes as a "primness" about lower-class people—that shaped the way he wrote about crime and poverty in the black community.[2] In *The Philadelphia Negro* he speaks often of the importance of distinguishing between the "better" classes versus the "idle and vicious," or at least "inefficient" and "undeveloped," within the Negro community. He divided the black residents of the Seventh Ward into four numbered "grades," placing "families of undoubted respectability" at the top and the "respectable working class" a notch lower. Below them, in grade 3, were "the poor," who were typically "honest, although not thrifty," with "no touch of gross immorality or crime." At the bottom were "the lowest class of criminals, prostitutes, and loafers: the 'submerged tenth'" who accounted for much of the city's crime problem, which Du Bois saw as both pervasive and growing.[3] A "significant change," he wrote, had come over the city's slums in the second half of the nineteenth century. "The squalor and misery and dumb suffering of 1840 has passed, and in its place have come more baffling and sinister phenomena: shrewd laziness, shameless lewdness, cunning crime."[4]

Du Bois backed up this observation with systematic scrutiny of the available statistics on the historical patterns of crime in the city—or, more accurately, the statistics on encounters with the criminal justice system, which Du Bois, like other early researchers, used as a rough proxy for actual crime rates in the absence of meaningful data on crime itself. Examining statistics on the racial breakdown of people sent to state and local prison, he concluded that black crime in Philadelphia in the decades before the Civil War had been widespread and very disproportionate in comparison to the city's black population. Based on statistics from the Eastern Penitentiary, where the most serious offenders were likely to be sent, Du Bois calculated that from 1830 to 1850 "less than one-fourteenth of the population was responsible for nearly a third of the serious crimes committed."[5] After a lull following the end of the Civil War, crime by both blacks and whites began to rise again, but the overrepresentation of blacks in the prison population continued. Again looking at serious offenders committed to the Eastern Penitentiary, Du Bois noted that "the 4 per cent of the population having Negro blood furnished from 1885 to 1889, 14 per cent of the serious crimes, and from 1890 to 1895, 22½ per cent."[6] Looking specifically at the pattern of offenses among the 541 blacks committed to the prison from 1885 to 1895, Du Bois saw particularly strong increases in robbery, burglary, and aggravated assault, including "assault to kill."

Du Bois knew better than to take these statistics at face value: he understood that statistics on arrests were the "crudest" measure of crime and could be no more than a "rough indication of the amount of crime for which the Negro is responsible."[7] He pointed out that the data on prison commitments could only be relied on to the extent that we accepted the assumption that they replicated "with a fair degree of accuracy" the amount of crime actually committed. And that assumption, he insisted, was "not wholly true": "In convictions by human courts the rich always are favored somewhat at the expense of the poor, the upper class at the expense of the unfortunate classes, and whites at the expense of Negroes." These biases necessarily had to "modify somewhat our judgment of the moral status of the mass of Negroes." But even "with all allowances," he conceded, there was "a vast problem of crime" within the city's black community.[8]

The questions then became what accounted for this "vast problem," and for its increase in the later years of the nineteenth century. Du Bois's answer centers on two things in particular: the adverse impact of racial discrimination, especially on young blacks, and the effect of the massive recent waves of black immigration. Part of the explanation for rising black crime was simply that crime in general was increasing in the cities after the Civil War, mainly as a result of the cities' growing population, the "increased complexity of life," and "industrial competition."[9] But there were also "special causes" behind the prevalence of crime for "the Negro," Du Bois wrote, causes that were both material and psychological: "he has lately been freed from serfdom, he was the object of stinging oppression and ridicule, and paths of advancement open to many were closed to him."

The "increasing number of bold and daring crimes committed by Negroes in the last ten years," Du Bois noted, had led to a "widespread feeling that something is wrong with the race that is responsible for so much crime."[10] But he argued that the real explanation lay in something within the larger society, not something wrong with "the race"; and its essential elements were not difficult to discern. The key was to recognize that crime "stands not alone" but is "the symptom of countless wrong social conditions."[11] And we could find clues to those social conditions by examining more carefully who was committing the crimes that so worried white Philadelphians. Looking again at the 541 blacks committed to Eastern Penitentiary, Du Bois pointed out that they were overwhelmingly male and young (more than 90 percent male and two-thirds under the age of thirty) and most often single. Only about one in five had been born in Philadelphia, with well over half coming from the South.[12] Many, especially among the more serious convicted offenders, were illiterate, or at least limited in their ability to read and write. Du Bois noted, however, that literacy among black offenders, as among black Philadelphia residents generally, had increased significantly over the past ten years and suggested that the growth of crime in spite of rising levels of education "shows how little increased intelligence alone avails to stop crime in the face of other powerful forces."[13]

What were those "other powerful forces" that drove black crime? To some extent, Du Bois suggested, they were the same ones that affected "poor and unfortunate" whites in an age of widespread economic insecurity and social dislocation—only more so, since blacks were even more often found among "the poor, the unskilled laborers, the inefficient and unfortunate, and those with small social and economic advantages." To that extent, he argued, there was nothing "new or exceptional" about Negro crime (or poverty). But beyond those "ordinary social problems" were "problems that can rightly be called Negro problems," ones that "arise from the peculiar history and conditions of the American Negro."[14]

The first of those "peculiar" conditions was slavery and its immediate aftermath. Du Bois placed special importance on the fatefully mixed impact of emancipation. Freedom from slavery had certainly improved the social and economic condition of blacks from what it had been before the Civil War. But much like any "sudden social revolution," emancipation brought mixed blessings. It created a "strain upon the strength and resources of the Negro, moral, economic and physical, which drove many to the wall." As a result, their economic and social trajectory in Philadelphia, as elsewhere, was less a steady upward climb than "a series of rushings and backslidings."[15] Adding to that precariousness was the mass immigration of Southern blacks to the cities, which had intensified competition for the "small industrial opportunities" available to blacks there.

But there was also another great force underlying Negro crime, which Du Bois thought was "possibly greater in influence" than the others: the "environment in which a Negro finds himself" in the contemporary city—"the world of custom and thought in which he must live and work, the physical surroundings of house and home and ward, the moral encouragements and discouragement which he encounters." The "strange social environment" of the Negro, Du Bois said, had to have "immense effect on his thoughts and life, his work and crime, his wealth and pauperism." And the core of that essential "strangeness" was white prejudice and resistance to black advancement—the "widespread feeling," not just in Philadelphia but "all over the land," that "the Negro is something less than an American and ought not to be much more than he is."[16]

The inimical environment created by white society had a multitude of impacts, all of which shaped the problem of crime in the black community. There was the "influence of homes badly situated and badly managed"; the "social surroundings which by poor laws and inefficient administration leave the bad to be made worse"; and, perhaps most important, the "influence of economic exclusion which admits Negroes only to those parts of the economic world where it is hardest to retain ambition and self-respect." Du Bois also called out "that indefinable but real and mighty moral influence that [either] causes men to have a real sense of manhood or leads them to lose aspiration and self-respect."[17]

Du Bois did not argue that "color prejudice" was solely responsible for the economic plight of black Philadelphians. But he did insist that it was a "powerful social force"—much more so than whites were able or willing to recognize. Systematic discrimination meant that even if a black man were well trained and "fitted for work of any kind," he "could not in the ordinary course of competition hope to be much more than a menial servant."[18] Things were very different for whites. "The young white man starts in life knowing that within some limits and barring accidents, talent and application will tell." On the other hand, "the young Negro starts knowing that on all sides his advance is made doubly difficult if not wholly shut off because of his color."[19] He could not hope to get supervisory or even clerical positions, "save in exceptional cases"; couldn't teach, except in a few "Negro schools"; couldn't become a mechanic or join a union. Even within the better-paid domestic service jobs, blacks were increasingly being replaced by whites. As a result, among other adversities, blacks "suffered more intensely the effects of competition and economic insecurity." Moreover, their children were routinely discriminated against in public schools and were "advised when seeking employment to become waiters and maids."[20]

Taken together with similar expressions of white prejudice in nearly every realm of social life, the cumulative impact was profound. "When one group of people suffer all these little differences of treatment and discriminations and insults continually, the result is either discouragement, or bitterness, or oversensitiveness, or recklessness," Du Bois wrote. "A people feeling thus cannot do their best." There were some exceptions, but blacks had been "so often refused openings and discouraged in efforts to better their condition" that many had essentially given up trying.[21]

Du Bois vividly described the long-lasting effects that this array of constant, predictable blockages and rebuffs had on personality and aspiration in the black community, and he provided rich examples from the lives of individual

Philadelphians based on his extensive field research. Under ordinary conditions, he said, blacks might wait more or less patiently for "color prejudice" and its effects to recede over time. But these constraints were too fateful and too urgent, affecting "matters of life and death"—threatening "their homes, their food, their children, their hopes." The result, he wrote, was "bound to be increased crime, inefficiency, and bitterness."[22]

The link between race prejudice and crime, then, was "neither simple nor direct." Crime was not just an immediate response to the denial of economic opportunity: "the boy who is refused promotion in his job as porter does not go out and snatch somebody's pocketbook." Rather, crime reflected the long-term growth of an "atmosphere of rebellion and discontent that unrewarded merit and reasonable but unsatisfied ambition make," along with a social environment of "excuse, listless despair, careless indulgence and lack of inspiration to work," which had been "built up slowly out of the disappointments of deserving men and the sloth of the unawakened." He summed it up with an eloquent warning:

> How long can a city say to a part of its citizens, "It is useless to work; it is fruitless to deserve well of man; education will gain you nothing but disappointment and humiliation"? How long can a city teach its black children that the road to success is to have a white face? How long can a city do this and escape the inevitable penalty?[23]

"Negro prejudice," in short, "costs the city something."[24] But Du Bois was unsure, at best, that white Philadelphians—and, by extension, white Americans generally—either understood those costs or had the will to do what clearly needed to be done in response. His argument is very much an appeal to the underlying goodness and rationality of white society, but it is also laced with both anger and a deep frustration, even exasperation. The facts and their implications for action were blindingly clear, but whites refused to act upon them, to everyone's detriment. "It is high time that the best conscience of Philadelphia awakened to her duty," Du Bois wrote. "Her Negro citizens are here to remain; they can be made good citizens or burdens to the community; if we want them to be sources of wealth and power and not of poverty and weakness then they must be given employment according to their ability and encouraged to train that ability and increase their talents by the hope of reasonable reward. To educate boys and girls and then refuse them work is to train loafers and rogues."[25]

Black Philadelphians, to be sure, also had a responsibility to tackle their community's problems, which were deep enough to call for a response that was "mighty and comprehensive, persistent, well aimed and tireless"—and reducing black crime was a crucial part of that communal obligation.[26] Du Bois emphasized again that black crime was often exaggerated and that it often reflected forces that were well beyond the black community's control. But that didn't mean that the community bore no responsibility for change. Creating a sense of aspiration and a belief in the value of work, he believed, was both possible and crucial to the black community's success. Still, Du Bois reserved his biggest criticism for the whites, whose attitude was typically both counterproductive and, ultimately, self-destructive. If whites failed to make a serious effort to do their part, the inevitable catastrophe would be no one's fault but their own.

Four years after *The Philadelphia Negro*, Du Bois elaborated these ideas in his extraordinary, poetic work, *The Souls of Black Folk*.[27] As in the earlier book, the problem of crime runs like a red thread through *The Souls of Black Folk*, and Du Bois again situates it as a predictable result of a combination of destructive forces: the corrosive effects of past slavery and current "race prejudice," and the failure of white society to step up to do what was needed to reverse those effects. But *The Souls of Black Folk* brings a sharper focus on the destructive impact of racial oppression in the harshly competitive, unforgiving economic system that emerged after the Civil War. The plight of black Americans in that context was summed up in one of Du Bois's most enduring lines: "To be a poor man is hard, but to be a poor race in a land of dollars is the very bottom of hardships."[28] That was true throughout the country, but it was especially applicable to a poor race in the particular historical circumstances of the post–Civil War South. And "the political status of the Negro in the South," Du Bois wrote, "is closely connected with the question of Negro crime."

Black crime had unquestionably increased, Du Bois noted, in the last thirty years; more disturbingly, "there has appeared in the great cities a distinct criminal class among the blacks." He attributed these developments to two causes. The first was the fact of emancipation itself—whose "inevitable result," he said, was "to increase crime and criminals." ("Under a strict slave system there can scarcely be such a thing as crime," he declared, though this was surely an exaggeration.) Emancipation had upended slavery's manifestly unjust but relatively stable social order—thereby pitching former slaves, who had been systematically made unfit for competition, into a brutal economy that had few supports for those who didn't keep up. Some people might do very well in that unaccustomed setting, but others would not: "when these variously constituted human particles are suddenly thrown broadcast on the sea of life, some swim, some sink, and some hang suspended, to be forced up or down by the chance currents of a busy hurrying world." This created a new kind of class system within the black population—ushering in "the beginning of the differentiation of social grades" among blacks in America and leaving the "incompetent and vicious" at the bottom. "A rising group of people are not lifted bodily from the ground like an inert solid mass, but rather stretch upward like a living plant with its roots still clinging in the mould. The appearance, therefore, of the Negro criminal was a phenomenon to be awaited, and while it causes anxiety, it should not occasion surprise."[29]

But the emergence of a "distinct criminal class" among blacks after emancipation also reflected a massive failure of social policy. Dealing mindfully with the newly emerging problem of Negro crime, Du Bois thought, should have been straightforward. Black criminals had begun not as hardened offenders but as people whose crimes "were those of laziness, carelessness, and impulse, rather than of malignity or ungoverned viciousness."[30] What they needed was "discriminating treatment, firm but reformatory, with no hint of injustice." But what they actually got in the post-emancipation South was almost the exact opposite: a "double system of justice" that "erred on the white side by undue leniency and the practical immunity of red-handed criminals, and erred on the black side by undue severity, injustice, and lack of discrimination." It was a system designed not for "firm but reformatory justice" but as "a means of re-enslaving the blacks."

The result was unsurprising: Negroes "came to look upon courts as instruments of injustice and oppression, and upon those convicted in them as martyrs and victims." This, in Du Bois's view, not only generated a deep suspicion and resentment of the (white) legal order; it also eroded effective social control in the black community. "When, now, the real Negro criminal appeared, and instead of petty stealing and vagrancy we began to have highway robbery, burglary, murder, and rape," the fact that blacks had lost all faith in the justice system had undercut the "greatest deterrent to crime, the public opinion of one's own caste." As a result, the collective sense of accountability shrank: the Negro criminal was now "looked upon as crucified rather than hanged." At the same time, the long-standing absence of concern for the rights of accused blacks and an increasingly unfettered and "savage" white response to real—or purported—black offenses exacerbated the already considerable pressures toward black crime. "Such a situation is bound to increase crime, and has increased it," Du Bois wrote. "To natural viciousness and vagrancy are being daily added motives of revolt and revenge which stir up the latent savagery of both races and make peaceful attention to economic development almost impossible."[31]

What could have been a manageable consequence of the dismantling of slavery was thus turned instead into a formidable social problem, through the violent imposition of a legal and political order that predictably bred "revolt and revenge." And that result was compounded by the mindless refusal of the Southern white establishment to make a serious effort to prevent crime in the first place by raising the social and economic position of the formerly enslaved population. Du Bois regarded the failure to invest in decent schooling for black children as especially perverse. He noted that four out of every five dollars spent on public education in Georgia went to white schools—which themselves were still mostly inadequate and "crie[d] for reform." How much worse, then, was the situation in the black schools? Yet there were powerful regressive movements in the South that wanted to gut Negro schooling even further. "What in the name of reason," Du Bois wondered, "does this nation expect of a people, poorly trained and hard-pressed in severe economic competition, without political rights, and with ludicrously inadequate common school facilities? What can it expect but crime and listlessness?"[32]

And beyond the failure to educate lay a much broader default. The very existence of the color line—which thwarted the best ambitions and dashed the hopes of even the most motivated—virtually guaranteed the flourishing of "inefficiency and crime." As Du Bois put it, "Draw lines of crime, of incompetency, of vice, as tightly and uncompromisingly as you will, for these things must be proscribed; but a color-line not only does not accomplish this purpose, but thwarts it."[33]

Central to Du Bois's assessment of the condition of blacks in the South at the turn of the century was his keen disappointment over the collapse of the promise of Reconstruction—embodied in the fate of the Freedmen's Bureau, which was established by the federal government in the wake of the Civil War but undermined politically and soon dismantled altogether. The bureau's efforts to radically improve the prospects of Southern blacks—through distributing land, opening opportunities for political participation, and providing accessible and effective public education, among other initiatives—produced real and transformative gains, for a while. But in a story that has often been told, the limited but meaningful gains of Reconstruction were largely erased by a combination of the withdrawal of support from the federal government and a deep and mounting intransigence on the part of Southern whites, which included a systematic campaign of violence and terror across many parts of the South.[34]

Du Bois was ahead of his time in grasping clearly the magnitude of the devastation that this reversal brought to black Americans' prospects. It cleared the way for decades of official discrimination, legally enforced deprivation, and state-approved violence, which not only harshly constricted the lives and opportunities of black Southerners but also stimulated their mass migration to the cities of the North and West, exacerbating the difficult urban conditions that Du Bois wrote about in *The Philadelphia Negro* and that scholars have continued to examine ever since. For Du Bois, the failure of Reconstruction was a hugely fateful case of missed (or, rather, deliberately thwarted) opportunity. It would not be the last.

II

The Souls of Black Folk was an impassioned and deeply personal statement, an extraordinary cry of pain and indignation as well as a call for action. Du Bois's central insight is simple and compelling: social peace and productivity cannot coexist with a harsh system of racial stratification. That kind of system will inevitably breed crime, and it is likely to call up an equally harsh—even "savage"—repressive response to the situation it has itself created. That insight was confirmed by scholars working in the decades after Du Bois—decades in which things became, if anything, even worse for great numbers of African Americans. In the South, the Jim Crow system hardened.[35] In the North, blacks—many of them fleeing from the bitter conditions in the South—became ever more concentrated in segregated cities with highly restricted opportunities. The Great Depression of the 1930s exacerbated these issues: though it had adverse effects on Americans of every race, it hit blacks with special force. Working within this deeply fraught social context, a number of innovative social scientists returned, in the 1930s and 1940s, to the kinds of questions Du Bois had asked, focusing especially on the consequences of living within a system that was profoundly hostile not only to providing economic opportunity but to fulfilling basic human needs.

One of the most influential of these explorations was the work of the Yale psychologist John Dollard. In 1935, Dollard went to live in what he called "Southerntown"— actually the small town of Indianola, Mississippi—with the idea of exploring the development of "Negro" personality under Jim Crow. But he quickly concluded that it was impossible to study Negro personality in isolation from whites, or from the larger system of what, following other social scientists in the thirties, he referred to as the "caste" structure of the South. He realized, he said, that "whites and whiteness form an inseparable part of the mental life of the Negro," who "lives by a set of rules which are imposed by white society." White and black lives were "so dynamically joined and fixed in one system that neither can be understood without the other."[36]

As Dollard and his colleague Allison Davis would later define it, "caste" in the American South was "a system for limiting social participation between color groups, and of thus differentiating between those groups with regard to the most fundamental opportunities in human society." It was in some ways like the class system that existed throughout the United States but also different in a crucial respect: its "arbitrary and final definition of the individual's status, a definition without possibility of change during his lifetime if the system persists."[37] It was possible, in other words, to move up and out of the class you were born into, but not to move out of your caste.

Caste and class were inextricably meshed, both in the South and, to a lesser degree, in the North. In Southerntown, as elsewhere in America, a class hierarchy—upper, middle, and lower—existed within each caste group. Dollard and other researchers in this tradition made it clear that the caste system was no accident: it was a scheme of both formal and informal domination deliberately designed to cement a rigid structure of privilege, which brought fundamental "economic, sexual, and prestige gains" to favorably situated whites.[38] (Notably, Dollard added, the white middle class—which was the biggest recipient of these gains—extracted them not only from the lower-caste blacks but also, to a lesser extent, from lower-class whites.) Whites gained economically by having almost exclusive access to the best and most rewarding jobs, while blacks were mostly confined to manual labor and "the most monotonous forms of work" and as a result got "a proportionately smaller share of the purchasing power of the community."[39] The whites' caste position gave them access to women of both races and also offered important psychological benefits—particularly "an automatic right to demand forms of behavior from Negroes" that served to boost whites' self-esteem and provide a "gratifying sense of mastery."[40]

Indianola gave Dollard an opportunity to study the caste system in its fullest expression. It was truly in the Deep South, in many ways not far removed from its history of large-scale plantation slavery, and anchored a county whose population was roughly 70 percent black. Poverty among both races was extreme, but it was deeper, more pervasive, and more consequential among the majority black population. A particularly telling statistic was that in Indianola and its surrounding rural areas the birth rate among blacks was far higher than that among whites, yet white families contained on average one more person than black families—meaning that a much higher proportion of black children were not surviving their early years.[41]

A central question for Dollard was how such an oppressive and manifestly unjust system could continue for so long. After all, its basic principles were fundamentally opposed to the core American values of democracy and equality of opportunity. And it was being imposed not on a small minority but on a group that in many places, including Southerntown, represented a majority of the population. Part of the explanation was that the caste system was enforced by the ever-present threat of both private and state violence that could be unleashed at any time, with brutal and sometimes horrifying results. The constant possibility of overwhelming repression, Dollard argued, profoundly shaped the black response to a situation whose patent injustice and deprivation had to be deeply frustrating and angering. It was, of course, possible for blacks to rise up against the caste system directly, and it had happened in the past. But given the huge power imbalance built into the caste system and the monopoly on legitimate force held by whites, such an uprising had never been successful—and had invariably brought down a massive and violent white reaction.[42] Blacks could also respond to the restrictions of the Southern caste system by leaving for the North, where caste certainly existed but in a much less rigid and pervasive form. Or they could adapt by achieving status, as best they could, within the class structure of their own caste, deriving gains of their own by moving into the black middle class. In other words, they could passively "accommodate" to the limits of their caste position; and many blacks, Dollard argued, did just that.

But blacks could also turn the aggression born of anger at the white institutions *inward*, toward their own community—a theme to which Dollard devoted a full chapter of his book. Central to this argument was the insight that feelings of hostility and rage generated by systemic injustice do not just go away. Instead, Dollard argued, in the face of the frightening consequences of expressing them directly against the people who have caused the injustices in the first place, those natural aggressive responses are deflected onto safer targets.

"The Negro individual," Dollard noted, "occupies a socially stereotyped caste position in which he suffers certain systematic disadvantages. He is aware of his disadvantages because he knows the difference between his actual status in Southerntown and his theoretical status as defined by the dominant American folkways and mores."[43] That fundamental contradiction creates frustration, and "the usual human response to frustration is aggression against the frustrating object." But in this case the frustrating object was the firmly dominant and inherently violent white caste. The question, then, was "what happens to the aggression which is inevitably germinated in this situation." And part of the answer was that "some of the hostility properly directed toward the white caste is deflected from it and focused within the Negro group itself." That response—by no means necessarily a conscious one—had two major advantages, according to Dollard: it allowed for the "biologically satisfying" expression of deep feelings of frustration, and it was "safer than taking up the hopeless direct struggle against the white caste."[44]

In linking violence among Southern blacks back to the caste system, Dollard was accomplishing two things of paramount importance to the understanding of violence within the black community. First, the idea of "deflected" aggression pointed to a structural understanding of violence as the result of white oppression, explaining that what might appear to be purely "internal" expressions of violence among blacks were actually traceable to the impact of white institutions. Second, this explanation challenged the dominant view in white society that regarded "excessive violence in the Negro group" as a "racial trait." Some of Dollard's white informants in the South believed that "Negroes are nearer to savagery" than whites; others attributed black violence to their inherent "emotional instability." Whatever the specifics, these explanations invariably saw violence as a quality inherent in the "Negro" race. In mild but telling language, Dollard countered that "a preferable view would seem to be that, since the hostility of Negroes against whites is violently and effectively suppressed, we have a boiling of aggressive affect within the Negro group."[45]

That "boiling" of aggression was compounded by another central feature of the caste system: the negligent attitude of the white caste toward violence *within* the black community, in stark contrast to the harsh and sometimes homicidal response to black aggression against whites. Dollard argued that this not only represented a profound injustice in its own right but that it was an essential part of the explanation for black communal violence. "It is impossible," he wrote, "to see the more violent patterns of Negro behavior in the right perspective unless one understands that there are different standards of justice for the two castes." Whites were usually (though not always) nonchalant regarding violence by blacks against other blacks; indeed, Dollard argued, they often benefited from the resulting discord within the black community. "One cannot help wondering if it does not serve the ends of the white caste to have a high level of violence in the Negro group, since disunity in the Negro caste tends to make it less resistant to the white domination."[46]

This tolerance of violence within the black community was not necessarily "a matter of conscious policy upon the

part of the white group"; it was more likely to be "prag-
matic, unformalized, and intuitive." But in practice, it
amounted to a "condoning of Negro violence" and gave
"immunity to Negroes to commit small or large crimes as
long as they are on Negroes." "Evidently," Dollard wrote,
again with studied understatement, "the whites did not
consider security of life and person for the Negroes a very
important issue."[47] Black lives, in short, really did not matter, at least not much, for whites in Southerntown. And that
attitude, Dollard argued, was "dangerous and destructive"
for the black community as a whole, even though it might
be regarded as leniency in any particular case.

Perhaps most fatefully, it meant that blacks, for the
most part, were forced by default into taking the responsibility for their safety into their own hands. Speaking of
a supposed tendency for lower-class black women to carry
"ice picks or razor blades" as defensive weapons, Dollard
suggested that the black community represented a "kind of
frontier, where the law is weak and each person is expected
to attend to his own interests by means of direct personal
aggression and defense."[48] Echoing the point made by Du
Bois a generation before, Dollard argued that the vacuum
left by the failure of the white system to offer basic protection led, over time, to an "idealization of personal violence,"
at least among some "lower-class" blacks—"an atmosphere
in which ability to defend one's rights or to be the successful
aggressor is highly prized." Though the middle class might
still value their position as law-abiding citizens, lower-class
blacks "do not appear to be at a social disadvantage in their

own class as a result of prison experience for a cutting or shooting affair" but were, if anything, envied for their "superior ability to take care of themselves."[49]

Some might feel that Dollard's analysis itself plays into stereotypes about black violence—and it surely would if it were applied across the board to the black community as a whole or if it were detached from its structural roots. But Dollard did neither. He acknowledged the reality of excess violence in poor black communities in the Jim Crow South, but then turned the traditional white explanation for that violence on its head. Southern black communities did suffer a great deal of internal violence. But this was not because black people were innately "savage" or inherently unstable or impulsive: it was a predictable result of the routine operation of the caste order itself, an expression of the "boiling" aggression that white domination and exploitation produced, exacerbated by white indifference to injury and violent death in black communities.

III

Dollard continued to explore the links between caste and violence in his collaboration, a few years later, with the African American anthropologist Allison Davis. Their 1940 book *Children of Bondage* made use of intensive interviews in New Orleans and the small Mississippi city of Natchez to investigate, in greater depth, the combined impact of caste and class on the "personality development of Negro youth in the urban south." Like Indianola, these cities were opportune places to study the psychological impact of caste because in them the caste system was pervasive—and extreme. In Louisiana as a whole, illiteracy among black adults was three times as high as among whites. New Orleans, which had the largest black population of any Southern city, also had the lowest average wages and lowest rates of home ownership among blacks. Just six out of every hundred black residents, versus nearly half of whites, held white-collar jobs. Although blacks totaled just a fourth of the city's population, "there were as many unemployed Negro adults in 1938 as white." At the same time, black women and children were far more likely than white ones to be in the paid labor force: the caste system, the researchers wrote, forced almost half of married black women to work, versus fewer than one in ten white women.[50]

In Natchez, where blacks made up roughly half the city's population, things were even worse. White families there earned, on average, almost three times as much as black families did; blacks mostly held only unskilled or domestic jobs. About a third of black adults were illiterate.[51] These harsh realities reflected an especially pure caste system that sharply divided blacks from whites "with regard to the most fundamental opportunities in human society." And short of moving away or of dramatic changes in the system (which were not then on the horizon), blacks in New Orleans and Natchez were stuck with it. As in Southerntown, an individual could move up or down in class within his racial group, but "he is born into his caste, and he must die in it."[52]

Davis and Dollard emphasized the wide variation of culture and personality within the black community. They never suggested that caste explained everything about black personality or that blacks' behavior was nothing more than a reactive response to it. But they did aim to show that caste was an inescapable force that powerfully structured black lives in the Southern cities—and, not least, that it helped to explain the high levels of aggression they found among Negro youth.

Davis and Dollard's research project interviewed over two hundred black youth and their parents in New Orleans and Natchez. *Children of Bondage* focused on eight of them in particular, ranging from lower class to middle class, in order to explore the central question: "What degree of character torsion does systematic oppression exert upon human personality?"[53] Davis and Dollard noted that six out of the eight youth they foregrounded in the book, both girls and boys, "exhibited unusually aggressive behavior in their schools and cliques."[54] And in tracing that aggression, in part, back to the caste system, they aimed to show in very personal ways that racial oppression had powerful consequences for human development. They directly challenged the common defensive view among whites that blacks were happy and well adapted to the Southern racial order. Their "thousands of pages of interviews" refuted the "widespread dogma" among whites that Southern blacks did not experience caste restrictions "as punishment," that they were "completely accommodated to their caste status and that they are simple-natured childlike beings with childish needs." Those beliefs were surely convenient for whites with a "vested societal interest" in maintaining their caste privileges, who needed to avoid confronting the "basic deprivations and frustrations which life in a lower caste involves." Against that self-serving ideology, Davis and Dollard argued that their research showed that "the sting of caste is deep and sharp for most Negroes"—deep and sharp enough to invade the most basic and intimate realms of family and personality.[55]

As in Dollard's analysis of Southerntown, *Children of Bondage* particularly highlights the ways in which the "sting of caste" was deflected inward, within the black family and community, because of the potentially devastating consequences of expressing resentment and frustration directly against whites. "At an early age," Davis and Dollard wrote, the black child

> learns that the economic and social restrictions upon him as a lower-caste person are maintained by powerful threats of the white society, and that any efforts to rise out of his caste position will be severely punished. Both in the city and in the country, the disabilities which his caste suffers are maintained primarily by a system of force. This superior physical and legal power of the white caste is not left to his imagination but is dramatized periodically for the whole society in the form of beatings and lynchings.[56]

It was also dramatized by economic reprisals, in the form of withholding work or wages. From both white people and his own family, the black child learned early on that "white people are extremely powerful and dangerous and that he must therefore not display aggression toward them."[57]

The result of this "torsion," as Davis and Dollard put it, was the suffusion of the black community by an unusual level of inward violence, both in the home and on the street—especially, but not exclusively, within the black lower class. Describing one lower-class youth they interviewed, whom they called "Edward Dodge," Davis and Dollard said that he "lives in an atmosphere of violence"— indeed, that he lived "on a sort of frontier of American life where the man with the most courage and the most invulnerable arteries survives."

As a child, Edward saw "many terrifying sights" and reported that he had recently come upon two men lying on the street near his home ground after a gunfight.[58] One of the men, shot in the belly, "eventually recovered"; the other "died on the spot." The researchers suggested that the boy "must have absorbed the lesson that he himself would grow up into a world of adults where shooting and killing would be a natural recourse in a quarrel, and he must not have been too frightened by it. After all, only one of the men died!" On another occasion, Edward saw a woman slash another with a razor on the street; the victim was seriously injured but also survived. "They took her to the hospital," the authors note, "and she *recovered*. The lesson again was clear: the manly or womanly thing is violence, and it is not so dangerous either."[59]

Davis and Dollard also presented the case of a fourteen-year-old Natchez boy they called "Judy Tolliver," who, like Edward Dodge, had both faced considerable violence— within and beyond his home—and dealt it out himself. Judy's father, according to an interviewer, ruled his house "by a reign of terror over each member of his family." He refused to let his wife see friends or go to church, and whipped her for talking with the researcher who inter-viewed her for the study. "Mr. Tolliver," the interviewer noted, also "makes a habit of whipping his children, regardless of their sex or age." He told the researchers that he sometimes experimented with *not* beating Judy, whom he regarded as "bad as he kin be," for as long as a week, but Judy just kept getting worse. His mother beat the chil-dren, too, until they got "too strong,"[60] at which point she turned them over to their father.

Even at fourteen, Judy was acutely aware of his position in the Natchez caste order. He lamented to the researchers that he "ain't never had nothing much," telling one inter-viewer that he "ain't never had but one $.50 in my pocket once what was mine to spend. I has always had a very hard time."[61] He was well aware that it was the white system that was mainly responsible for that hard time but under-stood that "I can't do nothing to the white folks that talks about kicking me but talk big back to them." Instead he took his feelings out on other black kids, and, especially, on "bright"—light-skinned—black people. As a child, Judy reported, he and his clique "was some bad and used to fight amongst ourselves all the time when we couldn't get nobody else to fight."[62] And now, he said, he "sure can handle colored folks who tried to act lak white folks just 'cause they is bright and got a little more money than some other colored folks":

> I shore do drop the wood on 'em and I don't feel bad over it . . . that is when I gets my feelin' out on 'em. I tries to kill 'em when I gits on 'em and see jes what good their color does 'em then. . . . They will pass po' people on the streets lak me and won't speak. I could jes' get somethin' and knock 'em in the head wid it. That is jes' why I be's so hard on 'em when I gits on one.[63]

Davis and Dollard's attempts to render the dialect of the lower-class youth they studied feel jarring to a twenty-first-century reader. But *Children of Bondage* does give some degree of voice to young people who, by virtue of their race, class, and age, were rarely if ever heard. And it presents those voices in the service of clearly linking what to whites were threatening, disreputable behaviors and attitudes to the insidious effects of an intolerable social situation that these children had no part in creating. The lower-class black child in the urban South, they insisted, was inclined to be aggressive not because black children were naturally built that way—after all, those better situated within the class hierarchy of the black community didn't behave the same way. Rather, "lower-class Negro children grow up to be fighters, cutters, and shooters" in the context of a world that is not only depriving and frustrating but is also "largely outside of the protection of the white law." In that context, it was also not so mysterious that parents would reinforce their children's reactive violence and, at the extreme, punish them if they *didn't* use violence to defend themselves. "The parent," Davis and Dollard wrote, "tells the child to strike out in defense of his body and to be certain to strike first." As one parent told an interviewer, "I tell Ernest to fight back, an' ef he don't, I'm gonnuh beat him myself."[64]

IV

Davis and Dollard made a compelling case that the Southern caste system bred violence among those stuck at the bottom—a grim counterpoint to the top-down violence that kept the system itself in place. But they had little to say about what, if anything, could be done to change that system and, in doing so, mitigate the violence it predictably generated. That may have been in part because they saw little hope for change in the caste system—unless, perhaps, you could chip away at the justifications for white dominance that helped to maintain it, which is part of what they hoped to accomplish through their research. A much more detailed analysis of the structure of white racial domination and the prospects for transforming it was not long in coming, however. It emerged from a massive social research project, directed by the Swedish economist Gunnar Myrdal, that began in the late 1930s and would culminate in Myrdal's landmark 1944 report *An American Dilemma: The Negro Problem and Modern Democracy.*

An American Dilemma, grounded in an astonishing amount of empirical research that exhaustively detailed the state of black America, devoted only a few of its thousand-plus pages to crime specifically. But one of Myrdal's key staff members, the University of North Carolina sociologist Guy B. Johnson, developed a monograph for the project on patterns of crime and punishment in black America. Most of it did not get published, but some of his views were set out in a 1941 article in the influential *Annals of the American Academy of Political and Social Science.*[65] Johnson built on the caste analysis of Davis, Dollard, and others and also provided original research of his own, to produce an argument that both reaffirmed the link between violence and racial oppression and highlighted the special contribution of the racialized justice system itself.

Like other serious writers in the 1930s and 1940s, Johnson began by explicitly rejecting any notion that black crime could be explained by something innate to Negroes. "We shall assume," he wrote, "that the fundamental causes of crime in the Negro are the same as in any other group and that the simple fact of race is not sufficient in itself to explain any important differences in criminal behavior." He thought that there might be some racial differences in "temperament or psyche," but he insisted that "by no stretch of the imagination" could those be "the primary determinant

of the amount or nature of crime." If we wanted to understand why groups differed in the levels and kinds of crimes
they committed, we needed to "inquire into their social
interrelations and into the ways in which their social envi-
ronments differ." And on that score, he said,

> the most important fact about the relation of the Negro
> to American society is his subordinate social status. In the
> South his social position is so rigidly defined as to consti-
> tute a caste position, and even in the North and the West,
> in spite of a certain amount of equality with respect to
> "civil rights," the Negro is generally subjected to social
> ostracism and economic discriminations.[66]

That subordinate social status, Johnson argued, was key
to the patterns of violence in the black community. In laying out this argument, he brought to bear a startling set
of statistics on homicide and its treatment in the courts
in several places in the South—Fulton County, Georgia
(which contains Atlanta); Richmond, Virginia; and five
counties in North Carolina. Johnson was most interested
in exploring whether murders were treated differently
depending on who was killing whom, and he expected that
homicides by blacks against other blacks would be treated
far more lightly than those involving black offenders and
white victims. That turned out to be true; but what most
jumped out from his data, as he pointed out, was the great
"preponderance of Negro in-group murders and the relatively small number of interracial murders." From 1930 to

1939, out of 220 indictments for murder in Richmond, 194 (88 percent) involved blacks killing blacks. The same was true of 75 percent of murder indictments in North Carolina. Of the 95 murder indictments in Atlanta across twenty months in 1938–39, 87 involved blacks killing other blacks, 5 were white killings of whites, and 2 were whites killing blacks. Only 1 involved a black perpetrator and a white victim.[67]

Like other observers from Du Bois onward, Johnson was keenly aware of the tendency of conventional criminal justice statistics to exaggerate racial differences in crime. But his own data were unambiguous: when it came to murder, at least, violence was startlingly concentrated within the black community. The question, then, was "what role does caste status play in the motivation of such offenses." Johnson's answer had several levels. He generally accepted the frustration and aggression thesis Dollard and Davis had put forward: for the black lower class in particular—the "lower class members of a subordinate race"—the "frustrations of being a Negro" were extreme. In a startling passage, he says of the black lower classes that "here one finds people who are utterly hopeless. . . . They have nothing and know that they will never have anything." And they "let off most of the 'steam' of their frustrated desires among their own group." A corollary of this, which Johnson thought was especially common in big-city ghettos, was the emergence of a "veritable society of their own" (what later scholars would call a "subculture") in which violence "becomes almost a positive value and has a high expectancy."[68]

Compounding the effects of extreme deprivation and hopelessness was the large and perverse influence of the justice system itself. Johnson was hardly the first to point out that a racist system of policing, courts, and prisons could contribute to high levels of crime. But he placed more emphasis than most on racist justice as a key causal factor in black violence and supported the argument with findings from his own original data on racial disparities in the disposition of murder cases in the South. Caste justice, he argued, exacerbated crime in multiple ways. To begin with, an openly hostile justice system could only lead to alienation, resentment, and a loosening of respect for law among blacks. The problem started with the police, who "pretty generally feel that in making arrests, handling witnesses, and obtaining confessions they can use brute force against Negroes with impunity."[69] In the courts, blacks went in with "the consciousness that the whole courtroom process is in the hands of the 'opposite race'—white judges, white jurors, white attorneys, white guards, white everything." And the frequent black experience of prison made things much worse. Southern prison systems, Johnson wrote, "are especially backward, and the caste position of the Negro exposes them to the worst which prison experience has to offer."[70] He listed a litany of well-documented evils: the "herding together" of young delinquents with "hardened criminals"; the special brutality of the chain gang system; the readiness of white guards to "use the lash, to use solitary confinement on starvation diet, and to shoot to kill." The consequences were predictable: "There is every reason to believe that the prisons 'graduate' an unusually high proportion of Negroes who have been brutalized and have become hopelessly bitter towards society in general and the white man in particular."[71]

But routine, systematized maltreatment was only one way in which a caste system of justice bred violence in the black community. Another was its negligence—its failure to protect Negroes from violence. Again, others had made this connection before, but Johnson brought fresh data to bear to support it. In Richmond, every one out of the five killings of whites by blacks in 1930–39 resulted in life imprisonment—versus less than 6 percent of the vastly greater number of homicides of blacks by other blacks. "To a considerable extent," Johnson concluded, blacks could "literally 'get away with murder' if they kill other Negroes."[72] The inescapable lesson, again, was that black lives really didn't matter very much to whites in the South of the 1930s. "The saying that 'Negro life is cheap' is tragically real, for even murder is sometimes condoned—one might almost say blessed—by the white man's machinery of justice." And that double standard, he wrote (echoing Du Bois's analysis in *The Souls of Black Folk*), "lends positive sanction" to violence within the black community.

In all of these ways, Johnson argued, the evidence suggested that "the administration of justice itself" was not only discriminatory—though it surely was that—but was also "a direct and indirect positive factor in the production of Negro crime."[73] He summed up his overall argument about the roots of black violence this way:

The position of the Negro in American society, with all that this means in terms of subordination, frustration, economic insecurity, and incomplete participation, enters significantly into almost every possible aspect of Negro crime causation. Indeed, it is so important as to constitute virtually a special and major set of sociological and psychological factors which can help "explain" Negro crime in so far as it needs special explanation.[74]

Two and a half years after the publication of Johnson's article, Myrdal's *An American Dilemma* reinforced this analysis, connecting the question of "Negro crime" to broader social and economic issues. Like many earlier writers, Myrdal began by noting that when it came to crime within the black community we couldn't fully trust the picture given by such official statistics as were available, since they represented an account not of actual crimes committed but of the encounters of Negroes and whites with the agencies of law enforcement. He acknowledged, however, that certain offenses were surely more prevalent in black communities. But he quickly dismissed the common assumption that blacks were therefore "endowed with a greater innate propensity to violence than other people." Instead, explicitly citing John Dollard's analysis of Southerntown, Myrdal argued that "the excess of physical assaults—and altercations—within the Negro community is rather to be explained as a misplaced aggression of a severely frustrated subordinate caste."[75] In the words of Ralph Bunche, one of the main contributors to *An American Dilemma*, many blacks faced with systematic oppression and discrimination might feel "fed up with frustration of their life here, see no hope and express an angry desire to 'shoot their way out of it.'"[76] But in a situation where, for the most part, "physical attack upon the whites is suicidal," black aggression "has to be kept suppressed and normally is suppressed"—or, at least within the lower class, "deflected" to other blacks.[77]

This was not just an issue in the South. Myrdal was well aware that the Northern version of the caste system also exerted powerful—and again thoroughly predictable— pressures toward crime. In an insightful passage on the appeal that illicit opportunities (what Myrdal called "shady occupations") had for urban black youth, he offered several reasons why it was "to be expected" that the black community "should be extreme in sheltering a big underworld." Chief among these was "the very great restriction of economic and social opportunities for young Negroes in ordinary lines of work, and the consequent experience of frustration."[78] That restriction of opportunity was all the more intolerable because it flew in the face of the nation's rhetorical embrace of egalitarian values—what Myrdal famously called the "American Creed." Indeed, he thought that black frustration was especially sharp in the North, "where educational facilities are flung open to Negroes, and public policy and public discussion are permeated with the egalitarian principles of the American Creed," but where those principles were rarely put into practice.

But the alienation of black youth did not result only from the denial of economic opportunity; it was also driven by everyday mistreatment. "The Negroes' respect for law and order," Myrdal wrote, "is constantly undermined by the frequent encroachments upon Negro rights and personal integrity, permitted in the South and sometimes in the North." Combined with "the general experience of exclusion and isolation," these made for "a fatalistic sense of not belonging. Quite ordinarily, the Negro is deprived of the feeling that he is a full-fledged participant in society and that the laws, in this significant sense, are 'his' laws."[79]

Overcrowding, poverty and economic insecurity, and the "great unemployment" of the Depression all fed into this toxic mix. And for Myrdal, this made recent trends in the economic position of blacks especially troubling. Writing in the midst of the wrenching transformations of World War II, Myrdal was convinced that many things were likely to get better for black Americans. Formal segregation, he thought, was probably on its last legs; white people's ability to maintain the caste system in its most extreme forms was unlikely to last in the long run, given the pressures of economic change, international opinion, black protest, and—not least—what Myrdal regarded as the basic goodness of most whites in a position of influence. The racist ideology of innate black inferiority that had propped up the caste system was, in his view, largely dying out. "The gradual destruction of the popular theory behind race prejudice," he wrote, "is the most important of all social trends in the field of interracial relations."[80] That was the good news. The bad news was that "the picture of the economic situation of the Negro people is dark" and the prospects for the future "discouraging"—primarily because of the specter of radically shrinking opportunities in the postwar economy for blacks to "earn a living by their labor."[81] The already dire poverty and economic insecurity of black Americans, in Myrdal's view, was likely to be exacerbated by the loss of traditional jobs—bad as they often were—in the agricultural South, due in part to the ongoing mechanization of farm work. Black workers, he predicted, would "continue to be pushed off the land and thus increase the number of job-seekers in nonagricultural pursuits." But at the same time, there were few new jobs to be had in the traditional "segregated Negro economy." This meant that blacks had to pin their hopes for employment on the "ordinary nonfarm labor market." But blacks had traditionally faced formidable obstacles in that market. They were kept altogether out of some industries in both the North and the South—even wartime manufacturing, where the need for labor was urgent. When blacks did get jobs in the "ordinary" labor market, they got the worst ones: mainly unskilled work, and those semi-skilled or skilled jobs that were "unattractive to white workers."[82]

So although in many aspects of life the trends were "definitely in the direction of a rise in the status of the Negro in America," Myrdal argued, "the same cannot be said of those relating to his occupational status." Unemployment was rising in precisely those cities, especially in the North, that blacks were fleeing to in order to escape a collapsing Southern job structure—which threw great numbers of potential workers onto "relief." Presciently, in the early 1940s

Myrdal already saw that from the point of view of the whites who controlled the economy, maintaining displaced black workers on bare-bones relief would be preferable to full employment. "The whole country, and particularly the North, was much more generous to the Negro in doling out relief to him than in allowing him to work and earn his bread by his own labor," he wrote.[83] W.E.B. Du Bois had noted essentially the same phenomenon almost half a century before.

Myrdal's hope was that the trend toward public economic planning that began (if haltingly) during the Depression and increased during World War II would allow the country to rise to the task of confronting what would otherwise be a deep crisis of mass unemployment after the war. "Large-scale public intervention," he wrote, "will be a necessity." In a passage that seems startlingly overoptimistic from the vantage point of the twenty-first century, he assured his readers that "in this endeavor no national administration will dare to allow unemployment to be too much concentrated upon the Negro." Instead, a combination of growing unionization, progressive legislation, and national economic planning would "tend to break down economic discrimination" after the war. Then, in what Myrdal called a process of "cumulative causation"—a kind of virtuous cycle—other kinds of discrimination would fall as well.[84]

Myrdal put the stark choices before America in language that at times was remarkably reminiscent of Du Bois. At the end of his report, he emphasized that "America is free to choose whether the Negro shall remain her liability or become her opportunity." The "Negro problem" was not only "America's greatest failure but also America's incomparably great opportunity for the future," and the nation's response would resonate beyond America itself. The right choice would send the hopeful message to the world that if we could solve *this* tough problem we could solve others too—that "peace, progress, and order are feasible."[85] If we wanted to seize the opportunity to fulfill classic American ideals, however, we could not simply "wait and see." We would have to "do something big, and do it soon." But that would require a level of "social engineering" that America, by comparison with some European countries, had lagged in accepting.[86]

Would America make the right choice? Myrdal wasn't sure. The kind of massive, national effort that he felt was urgently needed faced two stubborn obstacles: on the one hand, a lack of understanding on the part of whites; on the other, a bone-deep American resistance to conscious public social planning. The troubling economic prospects for black Americans were hard to change, in part because most whites were ignorant of the "total impact of what they have done to the Negro in the economic field." That ignorance called for a "deliberate and well-planned campaign of popular education." Myrdal had considerable faith that such a campaign could make a difference. But he was much less optimistic about the prospects for a concerted national effort to address the economic sources of racial disadvantage.[87] And given the strength of the economic and social forces arrayed against black economic opportunity, we could not rely on market forces to solve these problems. "The trend toward public control of the labor market," accordingly, was "the great hope for the Negro at the present time."[88] But how far that trend would go, in a society stubbornly resistant to public investment and planning, was anyone's guess.

V

It would be difficult to exaggerate the public impact of *An American Dilemma*: it had more influence on the way scholars and a wider public thought about race than anything written before, and perhaps since. It has been argued that the report helped to forge a "consensus" among scholars and policymakers about race relations in America that endured for at least twenty years after its publication.[89] And it is certainly true that it became a touchstone for decades of future thinking on race in America. It appealed, moreover, to a remarkably wide spectrum of readers. W.E.B. Du Bois himself described *An American Dilemma* as a "monumental and unrivalled study."[90]

To be sure, the report was not without its critics. Some challenged Myrdal's description of racial injustice as a "moral" problem in the hearts and minds of whites (language that did not, in fact, entirely convey the book's hard-headed economic analysis). Others, including the noted African American writer Ralph Ellison, lauded the book's direct challenge to racist ideology and to the complacency— even complicity—of much of American social science in the face of institutional racism. But they were troubled by what they saw as its tendency to regard black life in America as little more than a reaction to white domination, without independent agency or direction—the implication that black Americans were passively shaped by systemic oppression rather than active creators of their own lives.[91]

Myrdal's analysis of the economic obstacles looming for black Americans faced less of that kind of criticism, and it turned out to be remarkably prescient. But it did not lead to the kind of mindful and fundamental social action that he believed was indispensable for racial justice in postwar America. Nearly twenty years after the publication of *An American Dilemma*, Myrdal returned to the United States to give a series of lectures at the University of California, Berkeley, which were published in 1963 in a highly regarded book called *Challenge to Affluence*.[92] The book was a wide-ranging call for the United States to make better and more equitable uses of its unprecedented affluence, but it returned again and again to what Myrdal clearly regarded as the central paradox in American social and economic life: the continued exclusion of large numbers of Americans, especially Americans of color, from the fruits of the country's vast productive capacity. Contrasting the United States with most of the rest of the postwar industrial world, he pointed to a disastrous split between those Americans who lived in a sometimes bloated and "vulgar" affluence and a "large but mostly silent minority that enjoys neither security nor a decent standard of living."[93] The failure to address the rising problem of long-term structural unemployment was especially ominous: we were, he said, "on the verge of stratifying a substratum of hopeless and miserable people, detached from the nation at large." He warned of a "vicious circle" that was "well on the way to creating an 'underclass' of unemployed, unemployables, and underemployed, more and more hopelessly divorced from the nation at large and without a share in its life, its ambitions, and its achievements."[94]

More than half a century after *Challenge to Affluence*, the notion of an "underclass" has become both common and problematic. But Myrdal was apparently the first to use the term, and his use of it in the midst of the postwar "affluent society" was intended as a sharp critique of a larger American social failure. "The care and protection of human beings," he wrote, "and the improvement of their health, culture, and happiness, is generally less well provided for in America, particularly so far as the lower strata are concerned, than in the most advanced welfare states of Western Europe."[95] For Myrdal, there was nothing either natural or inevitable about the emergence of an American "underclass" in the midst of plenty, nor did the term imply anything derogatory about the people trapped within it. The underclass was a wholly unnecessary creation of wrongheaded public policies and the deeply flawed ideologies that supported them. Myrdal believed that the big structural trends in the US economy could be a source of unprecedented opportunity for everyone, as they were already for the majority of Americans, if we had the will and creativity to take control of them.

In a well-planned society, he argued, the "trend toward decreasing demand for labor in manufacturing and agriculture," in particular, should be seen as an opportunity, not a catastrophe. It meant that labor could be "released" from toilsome jobs to more rewarding and socially useful tasks. "Modern society should need less and less manual labor to produce the material goods that we need: more and more of our labor force could then be engaged in educating our youth and servicing our old people, preventing and curing illness, advancing science, and intensifying and spreading culture among the whole people."[96] The need to put future displaced Americans to useful work thus coincided neatly with the "very large volume of unmet needs in America crying to be met"—including "rebuilding its cities, clearing its huge slums, and reconstructing its obsolete and inadequate transportation system." Putting jobless people to work meeting those critical needs would address two of America's most pressing social problems at the same time. But this benign transformation would not "happen automatically as a result of the play of market forces." It would require "vigorous public policies" to create new jobs and give people the education and training to fill them.[97]

As in *An American Dilemma*, Myrdal saw those "vigorous" public measures as "a matter of the utmost urgency."[98] The longer we left people to waste in "underclass" conditions, the harder it would be to get them out. He worried that in an emerging economy that had little use for people with low skills, those unwanted workers would become "true outcasts" in American society. The line between them and those blessed with better preparation and better opportunities would become "almost a caste line"—because like the traditional caste system of the South, it would perpetuate itself across the generations. Long-term unemployment, Myrdal warned, was "a damaging way of life, particularly for the young, and above all when their educational and cultural level is low." The permanently unemployed lost much more than essential income: "such people become disheartened and apathetic."[99] Parents in that state could contribute little to their children's education, which was compromised in any case by the dismally inadequate schooling available to America's poor. Poor schooling and minimal investment in training, in turn, would render them less and less capable of filling the requirements of the emerging economy, leading to even deeper unemployment, and so on and on in a particularly insidious "vicious circle."

The progressive disabling of the "outcast" population was thus much more than just a practical matter of the loss of marketable skills, Myrdal warned. "The whole way of life of the urban and rural slums" would be increasingly destructive of "the will and ability to advance."[100] The longer people were exposed to the consequences of joblessness and poverty, the less effective belated measures to educate, train, and employ them would be. And we could expect crime and other expressions of demoralization to increase.

Would the country step up in the face of this looming emergency? As in *An American Dilemma*, Myrdal wasn't sure. In *Challenge to Affluence*, he alternates between his usual faith in the essential goodness and practical intelligence of the American people, and his sober awareness of the obstacles to social action—especially the "serious and irrational bias against public investment and consumption."[101] Myrdal appreciated Americans' philanthropic instincts, their willingness to give voluntarily for charitable purposes. But he thought Americans became "hardhearted and stingy" when it came to public provision and collective investment. He believed that political action sparked by the poor themselves might tip the balance. But as before, he worried that the traditional "muteness" of the American poor made that kind of bottom-up movement uncertain at best.[102]

VI

The human consequences of the missed opportunities Myrdal discussed in *Challenge to Affluence* were described in detail by a number of writers in the 1960s, of whom one of the most insightful was the African American social psychologist Kenneth B. Clark.[103] Clark had served as a staff member on Myrdal's *American Dilemma* project and afterward had become a highly influential scholar; his work with his wife, the psychologist Mamie Phipps Clark, on the psychological consequences of segregation for black children helped underpin the Supreme Court's 1954 decision in *Brown*

v. Board of Education outlawing segregation in the public schools. In the early 1960s, he was a key figure in the
development of an innovative community action program
in New York City, Harlem Youth Opportunities Unlimited (HARYOU). From that vantage point, Clark was able
to see up close the devastation wrought by the vicious cycle
Myrdal had described.

Working with a team of young researchers, Clark put
together a report, *Youth in the Ghetto*, based on extensive
interviews and observations on Harlem's streets.[104] Soon
after, he expanded those observations into the classic book
Dark Ghetto: Dilemmas of Social Power.[105] It was published
in 1965—a year after the federal Civil Rights Act had
been passed, and also just a year after the Harlem ghetto
had exploded in a weeklong riot, one of the first incidents
in what would be several years of violent urban disorders
around the country. Clark's analysis built on the work of
earlier writers from Du Bois onward. But it also brought a
deeper understanding of how powerfully the conditions in
impoverished black communities could affect the person-
alities of their residents—and, at the same time, a deeper
appreciation of the potential of ghetto youth themselves to
be active agents in transforming those conditions.

Clark saw violence and youth delinquency as among
many expressions of what he referred to as the "pathology"
of the ghetto. Harlem's homicide rate was almost six times
that of New York City as a whole; levels of narcotic abuse
were ten times higher; rates of mental hospital admission,

three times higher. All of these statistics and more, he said, were tangible metrics of "chronic, self-perpetuating pathology."[106]

In invoking the concept of "pathology" to describe Harlem's ills, Clark was treading on contentious ground. The term has a long and troubled history in American social science. It has often been used to pin the blame for poverty on poor people themselves—in effect, letting the larger society off the hook and implying that poverty can only be relieved, if at all, by changing the attitudes and behavior of the poor. But Clark's conception of "pathology" was very different. It wasn't the individuals living in the ghetto who were pathological, it was the ghetto itself—an institutional system that was deliberately imposed from the outside. And his central point was that imposing that system on human beings had profound consequences—consequences that were not pretty, but also not surprising. His book's emphasis on the pathology of the ghetto, Clark said, was meant to "describe and interpret what happens to human beings who are confined to depressed areas and whose access to the normal channels of economic mobility and opportunity is blocked." It was "not to be equated with assumptions of 'inherent racial differences' or with the more subtly discriminatory 'cultural deprivation' theories."[107]

Clark saw the ghetto as a holistic system of mutually reinforcing elements. At its core was economic exclusion, especially the historic confinement of most blacks, even in the North, to demeaning and poorly paid work. That economic reality, in turn, trapped blacks in poor housing, concentrating them in the ghetto. It also put huge stresses on families, as overworked and underpaid parents had neither the time nor the resources to adequately supervise their children. These obstacles were compounded by a history of systematic underinvestment in ghetto public schools, which led to poor skills and high dropout rates that—again, in a classic vicious cycle—helped to keep black youth trapped in the worst jobs. These realities—marginal jobs, stressed families, and poor schools—were not separate issues but strands woven into a single cloth. Nor were they a mere consequence of economic underdevelopment, which would naturally improve as the economy grew. Clark went further than most of his predecessors in calling out the processes that had created the ghetto as both systematic and deliberate. "The dark ghettoes," he wrote, "are social, political, educational, and—above all—economic colonies. Their inhabitants are subject peoples, victims of the greed, cruelty, insensitivity, guilt, and fear of their masters."[108]

Clark's conception of the African American ghetto as a kind of colony had multiple implications. It suggested that the racial ghetto was not just an assemblage of individual and institutional failures that could be easily touched up with a few conventional social programs. The ghetto was designed to exploit. It was no accident that its schools were routinely underfunded, its health-care systems minimal and often inaccessible, its police simultaneously abusive and unhelpful. And it persisted because the people who put it in place gained from having it there, and those who lived there were powerless to change it.

That overarching reality of powerlessness helped to explain the distinctive patterns of delinquency and violence that Clark and his HARYOU team had observed. Like Dollard and others, Clark zeroed in on the central fact that black violence was largely directed inward. "The victims of homicide cases in the ghetto and elsewhere are for the most part friends and relations, and not the feared and hated 'Whitey,'" he noted. "This may mean that the victim of oppression is more prone to attack his fellow victim than to risk aggression against the feared oppressor."[109] Being forced into an "inferior racial status," but simultaneously rendered powerless to do anything about it, led many ghetto residents to internalize a crippling and demoralizing sense of inferiority and self-blame, which helped to channel anger and a profound sense of injustice into self-defeating and often self-destructive responses.

The HARYOU team noted the aimlessness and lack of meaning of much ghetto delinquency. "Well, the gang, they look for trouble," one teenage boy told the researchers, "and then if they can't find no trouble, find something they can do, find something they can play around. Go in the park, find a bum, hit him in the face, pee in his face, kick him down, then chase him, grab him and throw him over the fence."[110] Ghetto homicide in particular, Clark wrote, often made no apparent sense; it expressed what he described as the "general purposelessness and irrelevance of constricted lives."[111]

That perception of ghetto delinquency as often reflecting

a profound obliteration of meaning and purpose—as a kind of "'nothingness,' without style or meaning"—sets Clark apart from other observers in his sense of just how deeply generations of racial oppression could affect personality.[112] But at the same time, his work with Harlem's youth had convinced him that their reactive anger and sense of injustice could be channeled toward more constructive purposes. "There is harnessable power to effect profound social change in the generally repressed rage of the alienated," he wrote.[113] His awareness of the damage wrought by racial oppression is balanced by his insistence on the potential strengths of oppressed people—their capacity for personal transformation in the service of social action. Since violence directed at other victims of racial oppression was itself a kind of thwarted rebellion, involving the young in a more focused and purposive rebellion could be a powerful alternative to the inward self-destruction that ghetto violence most often involved. Clark believed, in fact, that some kinds of delinquency, especially gang violence, represented small but significant sparks of inarticulate yet potentially constructive rebellion—a "desperate quest" for "a way of life of purpose and worth."

Clark, in short, saw the delinquent youth as not just a problem but also a resource. He contrasted this perspective to that of traditional social service interventions, whose "stated or unstated goal" was to help youth "adjust" to the constricted realities of their lives and thus to "function more effectively within the continuing pathology of his society."[114] It is fair to say that Clark viewed these goals as both illusory and immoral. On the other hand, he wrote,

> the value of involving or attempting to involve young people who are labeled as "delinquents" or "offenders" in realistic community problems and social action is two-fold: first, it could give them the types of insights and understanding of their predicament which might relieve them of the need to act out their frustrations in personal and self-destructive ways; and second, it could tap and channel the sensitivity and energy of the individual who has the ego strength to rebel by overt acts of defiance rather than succumb to apathy.[115]

The idea that oppressed youth could channel their rage away from mindless violence—directing it instead toward challenging the conditions that constricted their lives and deprived them of meaning and purpose—provided a sense of agency that critics often found missing in some of the earlier observers of violence in the black community. Clark had no illusions that this would be an easy process; he was keenly aware that bottom-up challenges to the exploitative power relationships that created and maintained America's ghettoes would encounter substantial opposition. But his insistence on highlighting the strengths of people—especially young people—who had typically been written off as either apathetic or irredeemably antisocial brought a new kind of hopefulness to the analysis of racialized violence, and one that remains crucially relevant today.

VII

Despite some differences, the pioneering observers of violence in black America, from Du Bois onward, all shared several remarkably similar insights. They all straightforwardly acknowledged that violence was a serious problem in many poor black communities, though they also took pains to point out that those communities contained a great diversity of social conditions, attitudes, and behaviors. All of them emphatically rejected explanations that invoked any kind of inherent racial proclivity to violence, whether biological or cultural, and instead firmly linked excess violence in these communities to the corrosive effects of white racial oppression. All of them, in fact, thought that given the circumstances in which many black Americans had been forced to live, whether in the North or South, violence was an altogether predictable outcome. And all of them regarded the links between racial oppression and community violence as complex and multilayered, involving not just the material impact of systematically blocked opportunities and enforced economic deprivation but also the deep psychological effects of pervasive racial injustice—the awareness that deprivation and restricted opportunities were conditions imposed from the outside by white institutions.

The overwhelming power of those white institutions, most of these researchers agreed, helped explain why black violence was so often turned inward toward other victims of a racist social order. And they also agreed that a racial double standard of justice, in which the protection of black lives was a low priority at best, exacerbated the problem by saddling many black Americans with the burden of defending themselves in a highly menacing environment—an environment made all the more dangerous by the threat of violence and harassment from police. Ultimately, all of these researchers believed, ending the plague of violence would require a fundamental transformation of the social and economic conditions afflicting much of black America. And every one of their insights, as we'll now see, has been affirmed again and again by more recent research.

FOUR

EXPLANATIONS, II: CONTEMPORARIES

The persistence of racial disparities in violent death and injury stands as a stark reminder of what we did not do—a testimony that the bold strategies against racialized inequality that Gunnar Myrdal and others proposed never took root. For a brief period in the 1960s and early 1970s, it seemed as if they might. The Johnson administration's War on Poverty, inspired in part by the work of Kenneth Clark and other scholars, pioneered innovative programs in job training, school reform, and community action. There was never enough money for these programs to come even close to meeting the vast unmet needs in America's cities, but they did reflect a willingness to acknowledge that the problems were very deep—and that serious help was well past due. The Kerner Commission pointed unequivocally to systemic racism as the root of the urban disorders of the 1960s, and called, among other things, for the immediate creation of a million new public-sector jobs.[1] But then the momentum stalled, and even reversed. Budget restrictions, caused in part by spending on the Vietnam War, and a decisive political shift away from the kind of conscious economic planning that Myrdal and others called for, doomed most of these proposals for structural change—and ushered in a period of austerity in public social spending that has been with us ever since. And beginning in the 1970s, the impact of those shifts was compounded by the rise of mass incarceration—which neither Myrdal nor anyone else had foreseen, but which would transform the fabric of life in many impoverished black communities.

A vast amount of research since then has illuminated the consequences of these choices. In a very real sense, it represents a record of opportunities not taken, a chronicle of possibilities not realized. It confirms that the excess levels of violent death and injury in black America result from deep structural disadvantages, whose specifics have shifted in some ways over the years but whose essence is remarkably persistent. As in the past, the research also shows that those disadvantages are a mix of both "ordinary" socioeconomic inequalities and the specific impact of what Du Bois described as the "peculiar history and condition" of black Americans—especially the "strange social environment" constructed by generations of racial discrimination. And it suggests that we will be stuck with these fundamental disparities in life and death until and unless we finally address those larger inequalities.

I

One of the most influential studies confirming the link between violence and racial inequality was carried out in the early 1980s by the sociologists Judith and Peter Blau.[2] The Blaus' analysis began with what they described as a "paradox": though crime rates are usually higher in poor countries, and America was an affluent nation, it suffered "one of the highest crime rates in the world." Its homicide rate was over ten times that of Western Europe, and its overall rate of violent crime had been increasing sharply since the 1960s.[3]

In seeking to understand the roots of that paradox, the Blaus theorized that interpersonal violence is far more likely under conditions of great social inequality—and that some kinds of inequality mattered more than others. In particular, what they called "ascriptive" inequalities— those based on "inborn" characteristics like race—were likely to be experienced differently than those based on people's varying skills or accomplishments, especially in a society where only the latter were supposed to matter. In a country "founded on the principle that 'all men are created equal,'" ascribed inequalities "violate the spirit of democracy and are likely to create alienation, despair, and conflict."[4] Inequalities based on immutable, inborn characteristics mean that for many people "there are great riches within view but not within reach," leading to "much resentment, frustration, hopelessness, and alienation." Violence, then, was not just a reaction to material deprivation. It was nurtured by the sense of "injustice, discontent, and distrust" generated by the highly visible reality that other people were doing better not because they were worthier but because they were, in this case, whiter.[5] As the Blaus put it, violence results "not so much from lack of advantages as from being taken advantage of."

The Blaus' emphasis on the special sting of ascriptive inequality harkens back to a key insight of writers like Myrdal, Dollard, and Du Bois: being poor is bad enough, but deprivation in a land of plenty, caused by racial distinctions that clash with the society's purported values, is even worse. It breaks the bonds that link people to others and to the values and rules of the larger society, and makes possible acts of aggression that would otherwise be inhibited. And the Blaus also shared something else with these earlier scholars: the idea that violence is not only a result of social and economic injustice itself but also of the absence of channels to challenge that injustice in more direct and potentially productive ways. Dollard and others had argued that the inward-turning violence in Southern black communities was not just a consequence of caste inequalities but also of the practical obstacles to doing anything about them through collective political action. The Blaus made a similar point. "A realistic reaction of the underprivileged," they wrote, would be to organize in order to "overthrow the existing order and redistribute resources or, at least, to fight for a larger share of them." But "the very differences manifested in great inequalities tend to deprive the lower strata of the strength and resources to organize successful collective action."[6] The result was what the Blaus, following the sociologist Lewis Coser, called "nonrealistic" conflict: "diffuse aggression, with people being more driven by hostile impulses than governed by the rational pursuit of their interests."[7] Individual violence, in short, represented a kind of partial and distorted substitute for a rebellion that, however justified, was out of the question.

The Blaus' empirical findings strongly supported this perspective. They calculated two measures of inequality—income inequality and socioeconomic inequality more broadly, which included education and occupational level as well as income—and tested how well these explained variations in the rates of violent crime across 125 urban areas in the United States. They found that the degree of income inequality and (even more so) broader socioeconomic inequality between whites and blacks powerfully shaped the levels of violent crime in urban America. The results confirmed their theory that extreme inequality engenders bitterness, disaffection, and "pent-up aggression," which in turn "find expression in frequent conflicts, including a higher incidence of criminal violence."

These findings deeply challenged some competing explanations of high rates of violence in black America. Lingering theories that linked black violence to genetic traits or other "distinctive racial attributes," for example, could not explain why levels of violence varied in tandem with levels of inequality. The Blaus' findings also undercut another explanation that had begun to gain some currency in the 1960s and 1970s: the notion that black violence reflected a specifically "Southern" culture that fostered higher levels of homicide and assault for all races. The South's "frontier" mentality and exaggerated emphasis on defending honor, in this view, made high levels of interpersonal violence predictable both in the South itself and among Southerners who had migrated to the North, as many blacks had.[8] The Blaus found that urban areas in Southern states did indeed have higher rates of violence, on average, than those outside the South. But they showed that when the different levels of economic and racial inequality in those cities were accounted for, the Southern factor basically disappeared. Southern cities had worse violence not because they were Southern but because they were more unequal in the ways that counted.

The Blaus' findings dealt a similar blow to the related idea that racial differences in violence reflected a distinctive "subculture of violence" within parts of black America. This theory had been developed most extensively by the University of Pennsylvania criminologist Marvin Wolfgang and an Italian colleague, Franco Ferracuti, in the late 1960s.[9] High levels of violence in a particular group or community, from this perspective, signaled the presence of a "normative system" that justified, or even mandated, the use of violence in interpersonal situations where the dominant culture would have forbidden it, or at least strongly disapproved. Wolfgang and Ferracuti thought they saw such a value system in many places: among the Sicilian mafiosi, the Thugs of India, and, most important, among some black Americans. Urban blacks, they argued, were "the current carriers of a ghetto tradition" that was passed down across the generations. In that tradition, "children inherit a subculture of violence where physically aggressive responses are either expected or required by all members."[10]

Wolfgang and Ferracuti's analysis was murky about exactly where that subculture came from: they conceded that "we are not prepared to assert here how a subculture of violence arises."[11] They did "forcefully" deny that blacks, or any other group, had a biological or genetic "proclivity" for violence, and at least hinted that the long-standing poverty and other adverse conditions under which urban blacks lived might have been responsible for generating the "subculture" in the first place.[12] But they argued that "over generations, poverty becomes a culture" with a life of its own—and it was that culture, not the adverse social conditions in themselves, that helped explain high levels of violence.[13] After all, they said, most people in deprived conditions didn't commit violent acts.

The idea that violence could be traced to a "subculture" that existed more or less independently of whatever conditions had initially brought it into being had important implications for what we could *do* about it. Wolfgang and Ferracuti were generally skeptical that directly addressing the adverse social and economic conditions in which many black Americans lived would make much difference. Instead, they focused on the need to attack the "subculture" itself—to "effect changes in the value system."[14] The subculture had to be "disrupted, dispersed, disengaged."[15] They suggested that ghetto residents should be literally "dispersed" more broadly throughout urban areas, in order to increase their exposure to middle-class values and decrease their exposure to the subculture. On the individual level, Wolfgang and Ferracuti called for something akin to reeducation programs, including "behavior modification" interventions, to implant conventional and presumably nonviolent values into people brought up in a subculture that extolled violence.

Blaming excess violence in the black community on its distinctive "subculture" appealed to the spirit of an age that was increasingly pessimistic about the potential of social action to improve the lives of poor and marginalized Americans. But it was also controversial, and for good reason. For one thing, as Wolfgang and Ferracuti themselves acknowledged, the theory came perilously close to circular reasoning: the fact that a particular community suffered a high level of violence was itself taken as evidence for the underlying cultural syndrome. Convincingly demonstrating that an enduring subculture of violence existed, and that it was heavily responsible for violence in the black community, would require direct evidence—some measure of the presence and strength of the subcultural values, as well as evidence that those values were resistant to change in the surrounding social conditions. But Wolfgang and

Ferracuti admitted that "basic evidence for the existence of a subculture of violence is still missing or tautological."[16]

The Blaus agreed. Their data, they argued, showed that there was no credible justification for invoking this kind of "subcultural" argument to explain racial disparities in the risk of violent death and injury in the United States. Existing economic and racial inequalities were sufficient to account for nearly all of the variation in levels of violence across America's cities.

II

Since the Blaus' classic study, there has been a great deal of careful research exploring the connections between inequality and violence. The research is often highly technical, and it is not all of a piece. But with stunning consistency, the studies confirm that the enduring racial disparities in violence represent what the Blaus called a "cost of inequality." And they drive home the hard reality that those inequalities—and their consequences—are still very much with us.

How much so is disturbingly apparent in a 2018 study exploring rates of homicide in eighteen US cities from 1999 through 2013—a time, again, when the country was widely said to be enjoying an unprecedented "crime decline."[17] Focusing on trends in homicide in these cities at the neighborhood level, the sociologist Lauren Krivo and her colleagues found three distinct patterns. Many neighborhoods enjoyed low and declining rates of homicide during those years; another sizable group saw rates that were "moderate" and stable. But a third, smaller group of neighborhoods suffered homicide rates that were both high and increasing. And these differing patterns were overwhelmingly shaped by race. Of the neighborhoods that suffered high and increasing homicide rates, fully 94 percent were predominantly black. Not all black neighborhoods fit this pattern of high and rising homicide: indeed, about a third of them were in the low-and-declining-homicide-rates category, and the high-and-rising rates were found in only about another third. But nothing remotely comparable was seen in any communities that were mostly white.[18]

Seeking to understand the sources of what they called the "durability of ethnoracial inequality in crime," Krivo and her colleagues developed a multidimensional measure of "disadvantage," which included joblessness, the proportion of people employed in low-wage jobs, the proportion of families headed by a single parent, the percentage of adults who were high school graduates, and the local poverty rate. They found that communities that scored high on this measure were much more likely to suffer high and rising rates of homicide.[19] Blacks were much more likely to live in the neighborhoods where disadvantage was worst, so this measure went a long way toward explaining the overwhelming presence of black communities among those with increasing numbers of violent deaths. But even with this measure of disadvantage accounted for, the proportion of black residents in a neighborhood seemed to be independently connected to higher levels of homicide.

That is a common finding in recent research, and considerable effort has been devoted to trying to figure out what it means. The resulting dialogue has illuminated a great deal about the specific ways in which race and violence continue to be linked in America. On balance, it confirms the dual insights of Du Bois and the Blaus: first, that the excess levels of violence in parts of the black community reflect deep and continuing structural disadvantages; and second, that there is something *especially* destructive about the kind of structural disadvantages that have historically been—and continue to be—experienced by many black Americans. The theory of a distinctive subculture that encourages (or even mandates) interpersonal violence has not fared well under hard scrutiny. But the notion that blacks are uniquely subject to a particularly toxic array of adverse circumstances has found significant empirical support.

The uniqueness of adversity faced by black Americans can be seen in several studies that address what has often been called the "racial invariance" thesis—the idea that, as the sociologists Robert J. Sampson and William Julius Wilson put it in an influential 1995 paper, the sources of crime are "remarkably invariant across race and rooted instead in the structural differences among communities."[20] Put simply, if you placed blacks, whites, Asians, Hispanics, or any other group in the same structural conditions, you would expect to see the same levels of violence in response. Hence the only reason for the extreme levels of violence among some black Americans is that they are found disproportionately in communities of extreme social disadvantage. If whites lived in the same kinds of communities, the "racial invariance" thesis suggests, they would have the same levels of violence.

This perspective is a useful corrective to simplistic theories that propose to explain violence as the result of a unique racial or ethnic subculture. But it may not tell the whole story. Part of the problem is that in the American context, blacks and whites are almost never *in* the same structural conditions. In order to test whether economic and social deprivation fully explains the racial differences in violence, we would need to compare highly deprived white communities with highly deprived black ones, to see if, in fact, they suffer the same degree of violence. But finding white communities that match the level of deprivation that is all too common in black America is nearly impossible.

That is one of the most important takeaway points from a classic 1996 study that Krivo and her colleague Ruth Peterson carried out in Columbus, Ohio—at the time, one of the few major cities in the United States with a substantial number of highly disadvantaged white communities.[21] "Examining poverty, disadvantage, and crime in a city where extreme community poverty and disadvantage are not synonymous with black neighborhoods," Krivo and Peterson wrote, "tests the argument that local structural conditions (rather than race/culture) are important determinants of crime."[22] They studied 177 local census tracts in Columbus, dividing them into ones with "low" poverty (meaning that less than 20 percent of their residents were below the official federal poverty level), "high" poverty (20 to 30 percent below the poverty level), and "extreme" poverty (40 percent or more residents living below the poverty level). Nearly two in five mostly black census tracts fit the "extreme" poverty designation, versus just 7 percent of mostly white neighborhoods. But in absolute terms, since there were many more white neighborhoods in Columbus overall, there were roughly as many "extremely poor" white tracts as black ones, which made a comparison of levels of violence meaningful.

In addition to poverty, Krivo and Peterson also looked at male joblessness, family disruption (as measured by the proportion of families without a male head of household), and the proportion of residents aged sixteen or over in professional occupations (which they argued was a measure of the presence of middle-class role models). They then examined the effects on violence of those four factors, both individually and when taken in combination as an index of overall disadvantage. All four measures were associated with higher rates of reported violent crime. But what stood out most sharply was the stark difference between extremely disadvantaged communities and all the others. The gap in violence between communities suffering "extreme" deprivation and those where deprivation was ranked as "high" but not "extreme" was usually much wider—often dramatically wider—than that between "high" and "low" deprivation neighborhoods. Krivo and Peterson concluded that violence "is especially escalated when disadvantage is particularly widespread" and particularly severe.[23] Beyond a certain level of poverty, joblessness, and other disadvantages, the nature of community life underwent a sharp, qualitative change.

Because white poverty was relatively common in Columbus, Krivo and Peterson were able to show that this qualitative change happened in white communities as well as black ones. In white census tracts where levels of poverty, female-headed families, and the combined index of disadvantage were "extreme," violence was dramatically higher than in white areas with "high" levels of disadvantage. The same processes, in other words, seemed to be operating in white neighborhoods as well as black ones. Within either race, higher levels of community disadvantage predictably generated higher levels of violence, especially when disadvantage passed a certain threshold and became "extreme." And the degree of disadvantage explained a very substantial proportion of the overall variation in violence across Columbus's census tracts.

Krivo and Peterson took this as basically an affirmation of the racial invariance argument, and that is how their study has been generally viewed ever since. But as the researchers themselves acknowledged, things were actually not so clear-cut. Rates of violence remained higher in the hardest-hit black communities than in the hardest-hit white ones, and the racial composition of a census tract seemed to have some independent effect on violence over and above the level of structural disadvantage. So although the links between adverse structural conditions and violence held across communities of whatever race, they didn't explain *all* of the stark racial disparities in violence in Columbus. Indeed, the fact that there were so few American cities with enough extremely poor white communities to make this sort of comparison possible at all may be the study's most telling finding. Even in Columbus, with its close proximity to Appalachia, one of the heartlands of white poverty in America, only 9 out of 123 predominantly white census tracts—versus 10 of 26 predominantly black ones—could be characterized as "extremely" disadvantaged. That the few white people living in circumstances dire enough to *almost* match those of the most deprived black communities suffer *almost* as much violence does tell us something important about the power of extreme social circumstances to affect people's lives, whatever their race or ethnicity. But the fact that so few whites actually do live in such conditions tells us something at least as important. In the abstract, people of any race can be pushed into conditions that place them at very high risk of violent death or injury. In the real world, that situation is rare for white Americans. And the difference, of course, is not accidental.

A look at cities other than Krivo and Peterson's carefully chosen example of Columbus drives home the point. A few years after their study, for example, the University of Georgia criminologist Thomas McNulty studied the link between disadvantage and reported violent crime in Atlanta, a majority black city with a large African American middle class.[24] Like Krivo and Peterson, McNulty used a multidimensional measure of disadvantage, which included the percentage of people with incomes below poverty level, the percentage of families with children headed by a single woman, and the percentage of men over the age of sixteen who were officially unemployed or out of the labor force. The goal was to explore whether communities at similar levels of disadvantage, regardless of race, suffered similar levels of violent crime. But there was a fundamental obstacle: only 1 out of 107 mostly white areas in Atlanta scored significantly above the city's average level of disadvantage, while 104 out of 245 mostly black areas did. No white areas, moreover, were *far* above the average level of disadvantage, while 48 of the largely African American areas were. The highest levels of disadvantage in white Atlanta neighborhoods never came anywhere near those in the city's most deprived black neighborhoods. McNulty found that the level of disadvantage did have a strong effect on the amount of violence in black neighborhoods: those that were highly disadvantaged suffered between two and two and a half times as much violence as those with low levels of disadvantage. But it was impossible to determine whether levels of violence would be equally high in very heavily disadvantaged white communities, because there were virtually no heavily disadvantaged white communities to study—at least none that came close to matching the most deprived black communities. McNulty called this a problem of "restricted distributions," meaning that the distribution of blacks and whites across the spectrum of social advantage and disadvantage is so different that most of the time we can't even make meaningful comparisons between them.

Since there were substantial numbers of both black and white neighborhoods with relatively *low* disadvantage in Atlanta according to McNulty's measure, it was still possible for him to explore whether racial disparities existed across *those* communities. And contrary to the prediction of the "racial invariance" argument, they did. In relatively low-disadvantage areas in Atlanta that were mostly black, homicide rates were roughly four times higher than in comparable white areas, while rates of reported rape and assault were more than twice as high. As with Krivo and Peterson's Columbus study, then—only more starkly— McNulty's work suggests that the experience of blacks is both worse and, in crucial ways, different from that of whites. Broad economic and social circumstances explain much of the disparity in violence between the races, but they do not explain all of it.

But what does? Confronted with this question, some researchers have tried reviving the idea that hard-to-measure "cultural factors" may be at work. The Rutgers University sociologist Julie Phillips, for example, made this argument on the basis of a study of homicide rates among whites, blacks, and Latinos in 129 metropolitan areas across the country. Phillips found that the racial and ethnic differences in homicide across these metropolitan areas were extreme: the black rate was roughly eight times higher than the rate for whites, with the Latino rate in between, though closer to the rate for whites. Not surprisingly, those disparities closely paralleled racial and ethnic differences in key social indicators, including poverty, interracial economic inequality, and male unemployment. Black male unemployment was about one and a half times higher than the Latino rate and about triple the white rate. Over 17 percent of black families in these urban areas fell below the poverty line, with Latino families, at more than 16 percent, not far behind; less than 4 percent of white families, on the other hand, were in poverty.

Phillips showed that those social conditions mattered greatly in explaining racial and ethnic disparities in violent death—but more so for Latinos than for blacks. If urban Latinos shared the same favorable structural conditions as whites, she calculated, they would actually have a *lower* homicide rate than whites did. But structural conditions explained only about 57 percent of the black/white difference in homicide—meaning that if urban blacks shared the same structural conditions as whites, their homicide rate, though it would fall significantly, would still exceed that of whites. The persistence of this racial gap, Phillips speculated, was "due to the interaction between structural and unmeasured cultural factors."[25]

A similar suggestion appears in a more recent study by Darrell Steffensmeier and his colleagues, who studied arrest rates for homicide and other violent crimes in California and New York, two states with large Hispanic populations. Like Phillips, they found that the ethnic and racial differences in violence were startling. During the three years from 1999 through 2001, the black homicide rate in these states was between five and six times the white rate and two and a half times the Latino rate. An overall violence index—combining homicide, robbery, rape, and aggravated assault—was four times higher for blacks than for whites, and, again, two and a half times higher for blacks than for Hispanics.[26] Measures of disadvantage (including poverty, unemployment, the lack of a high school education, and number of single-mother families) strongly correlated with the rates of both homicide and overall violence in all three groups—whites, blacks, and Latinos. But while disadvantage *helped* to explain the difference in rates of violent arrests in the various communities, it didn't explain *all* of it. And as in Phillips's study, this was particularly noticeable when it came to differences in violence between blacks and Hispanics. Steffensmeier and his colleagues concluded that "racial/ethnic disparities in levels of disadvantage are only part of the story regarding racial/ethnic differences in violent offending." Another part, they suggested, might be that "cultural differences between structurally similarly situated residents might result in sharply different crime/violence patterns."[27]

These speculations echo, in more moderate form, Wolfgang and Ferracuti's "subculture of violence" theory, and they are shared by some other recent researchers. But assuming that the "unexplained" part of the racial disparity in violence reflects something peculiar to black culture overlooks the fact that these different groups might not really be "similarly situated" after all.

For one thing, the broad-brush measures of disadvantage

typically used in these studies fail to capture certain ways in which conditions of life in some black communities are substantially different from those almost anywhere else. Consider poverty, for example. The measure that researchers most often used to control for whether blacks and whites live in the same poverty-stricken conditions is the proportion of people whose incomes are below the federal government's official poverty level—a useful measure as far as it goes, but one that tells us nothing about the severity or depth of their poverty, or how long it lasts. And the racial differences on those counts are telling. Black Americans, for example, are almost three times as likely to be living on incomes that are less than half the poverty level as whites.[28] And it is arguably that kind of "deep" poverty, not simply the proportion of people below the poverty line, that is likely to have the most impact on violence.

Racial differences in the *persistence* of poverty over time may be even more important. The conventional measure of poverty treats it as a fixed condition: you are either poor or you are not. But most people whose income puts them below the poverty level at any given point will move out of poverty, many of them sooner rather than later—while others will be mired in poverty for years or decades, or for life. And data from the US Census Bureau's Survey of Income and Program Participation (SIPP) illuminate how strongly these differences are patterned by race. Rather than measuring poverty at one point in time, the SIPP follows the experience of households from month to month over the course of three years, giving a more dynamic portrait of the contours of American poverty. For example, the SIPP shows that over the course of three years, about 32 percent of the overall American population falls below the poverty line for a period of at least two months (what the survey calls a "spell" of poverty)—more than double the number counted as poor by the official poverty measure. A much smaller proportion, less than 4 percent, suffer "chronic" poverty—meaning that they stay poor for *all* thirty-six months. And chronic poverty is strikingly skewed by race—affecting 1.4 percent of Asians and 2 percent of non-Hispanic whites, but over 6 percent of Hispanics and almost 9 percent of African Americans.[29]

Blacks, then, are not only more likely to be poor but also more likely to be *very* poor, to stay poor for a longer time, and to be less able to escape poverty at all. And the SIPP also points to another way in which the conventional measures used by researchers miss a great deal of what is arguably important in understanding the links between deprivation and violence. It enumerates a number of specific "hardships" that are not measured in the federal poverty count but that indicate a household's difficulty in fulfilling "basic needs"—namely, "difficulty meeting essential expenses, not paying rent or mortgage, getting evicted, not paying utilities, having utilities cut off, not seeing a doctor when needed, not seeing a dentist when needed, and not always having enough food."[30] Most American households manage to avoid these hardships, most of the time. But many do not, and risk of falling behind on basic needs is, again, sharply skewed by race. In 2011, 35 percent of black households suffered at least one of these hardships, versus 30 percent of Hispanics and just 18 percent of whites. Over 10 percent of black households suffered *three or more* of these hardships during the year, more than double the rate for non-Hispanic whites.

When we look more closely at the nature of poverty and hardship, then, it becomes clear that the experience of blacks in America has been distinctly different, often dramatically so, from that of whites—and even, to a lesser degree, from that of Hispanics—in ways that are frequently missed by our usual measures of poverty and disadvantage. This isn't to minimize the degree of hardship faced by many people of *every* race and ethnicity in the United States in the twenty-first century: we are, as Gunnar Myrdal lamented sixty years ago, a conspicuous outlier among advanced industrial nations in the level of deprivation that we tolerate. But the black experience in this regard is extreme. And this matters in helping to explain why rates of violent death and injury are higher in some black communities than in white and Latino communities that, on the surface, appear statistically similar.

III

Conventional measures of social disadvantage obscure the scope and depth of adversity in many black communities in another way as well: they don't account for all of the multiple and mutually reinforcing ways in which generations of discrimination and segregation have shaped black lives. Poverty and the lack of good work are crucial and consequential hardships. But so are dysfunctional, dilapidated schools, unsafe and unaffordable housing, inaccessible or inadequate health care, negligent and abusive policing, and lack of political representation or voice—as well as the everyday insults and obstacles that are an inescapable and enduring part of life in racially segregated communities. And a growing body of research shows that these adversities are also linked to racial disparities in violence, extending and compounding the impact of extreme economic disadvantage.[31]

This synergy helps explain the frequent finding that racial segregation has an independent impact on community violence—and that the combination of economic adversity and racial segregation is more closely linked to violence than either of them alone. A compelling illustration comes from a recent study of violence in Massachusetts by Nancy Krieger and her colleagues at the Harvard School of Public Health.[32] Looking at the years from 1995 to 2010, they found "stark" racial differences in both fatal and nonfatal violence. Though blacks were only 6 percent of Massachusetts's population during these years, they suffered 40 percent of its homicides overall, and over 50 percent of its homicides committed with firearms. For nonfatal assaults, the picture wasn't much better: blacks accounted for well over a third of them, and, again, for more than half of those committed with guns. To explore the social roots of these disparities, Krieger and her colleagues measured the effects of economic disadvantage and racial segregation independently, as well as the effect of what they called "racialized economic residential segregation"—meaning the concentration of people with both low income *and* "low racial privilege" (in this case, blacks) within census tracts across the state. Both economic disadvantage and racial segregation, they found, were significantly related to violence in their own right. But the combination of the two of them had the strongest impact.[33]

And that finding isn't confined to Massachusetts. The special significance of segregation appears on the national level as well, as shown by a 2009 study of violent crimes in seventy-nine cities across the United States.[34] Again, the aim was to see whether, and how much, the degree of racial segregation *added* to the explanation of variations in violence, over and beyond the impact of structural disadvantage. The researchers pointed out that living under the impact of segregation is the usual condition for black Americans, more than three out of five of whom live in highly segregated communities—far more than any other group. They compared the rates of homicide, rape, and robbery reported to the police with a measure of "disadvantage" similar to ones we've seen before, which included factors such as joblessness, poverty, school dropout rates, number of female-headed families, and percentage of people working in very low-wage jobs. The researchers also added a measure of neighborhood segregation.

Like much other research, this study found that neighborhoods with more disadvantage suffered dramatically higher levels of violence. But beyond that familiar effect, the study also found that neighborhood violence was "significantly higher in more highly segregated cities." And though disadvantaged black neighborhoods were the most negatively affected by a city's higher level of segregation, the adverse effects of segregation "spilled over" beyond them. White communities, as usual, did not come even close to the levels of violence that prevailed in high-disadvantage black neighborhoods. But no neighborhood was immune from the overall effect of racial segregation. Segregation, the researchers found, created "conditions conducive to higher levels of violence in local communities of all colors and compositions." Residential segregation, in that sense, had become "everyone's problem."[35]

But why might segregation have an independent effect on violence, over and above the well-known impact of social and economic disadvantage? The research suggests several ways in which this might happen. Most generally, segregation matters because it is a marker for many other adversities—a kind of shorthand for the whole range of historical and current patterns of deliberate discrimination and disinvestment that have profoundly shaped black life in America. And for blacks who do manage to move up the social and economic ladder, segregation creates barriers to residential mobility, making it harder for them to escape violent surroundings despite their socioeconomic success.

This last point is highlighted in a study by Elizabeth Griffiths that explores the effects of poverty and segregation in Buffalo, New York, from the 1950s through the 1990s.[36] Like many cities in postindustrial America, Buffalo was hit hard by the decline of traditional manufacturing employment during this period. It was also "hyper-segregated"—meaning that as late as 1990, virtually all black residents lived in mostly black neighborhoods, and nearly as large a proportion of whites lived in neighborhoods that were almost entirely white. The proportion of black residents, moreover, increased sharply over the second half of the twentieth century. Blacks made up just 4 percent of Buffalo's population in 1950 but 29 percent in 1990. The level of poverty in the city fell from 1950 to 1970, following the trend of the United States as a whole, but rose sharply thereafter—from about 14 percent of Buffalo's residents in 1970 to 26 percent by 1990. And as the city got blacker and poorer, it also became deadlier. The average homicide rate in Buffalo rose almost sevenfold between the 1950s and the 1990s, and the gap between neighborhoods with high rates of violence and those with low rates widened as well.

Griffiths wanted to know how much segregation itself helped account for the distribution of homicides across Buffalo's neighborhoods and the way in which it had spread through the city over the fifty-year span. Like other researchers, she expected that poverty and other structural conditions alone would explain much of the distribution and trajectory of homicide rates over time, and that turned out to be true. A "poverty-related" index (which included rates of poverty, the percentage of males age sixteen and over not in the labor force, the percentage of homes that were not owner occupied, and the percentage of residents who had not finished high school) accounted for a very substantial part of the variation in homicides across Buffalo's neighborhoods throughout most of the period. But adding local racial segregation explained even more. Moreover, segregation's independent effect increased over the fifty-year period—meaning that over time, the poverty index alone became less predictive of a neighborhood's level of homicide.

That was not because poverty, low education, and joblessness ceased to be important factors driving Buffalo's homicide rate. Instead, it reflected the fact that over time, even the city's higher-income black neighborhoods became more vulnerable to violence. Though homicides spread to new areas of the city over the half-century, they remained concentrated in "clusters" of heavily African American neighborhoods. Even those black neighborhoods that had relatively higher incomes were more likely to be in, or adjacent to, those high-violence clusters, which made them vulnerable to a "crime spillover" effect. Griffiths concluded that Buffalo's black neighborhoods, whatever their class level, suffered from a "spatial precariousness" that set them apart from white neighborhoods with similar socioeconomic characteristics.[37]

What's crucial to understand is that this kind of spatial precariousness is neither random nor accidental. It is the product of deliberate social policies, at both the local and the national levels, that not only tolerated racial segregation but actively helped to create and maintain it.[38] In the 1930s, the Home Owners' Loan Corporation—an agency created by the Franklin D. Roosevelt administration—published maps to assist banks and other financial institutions in determining which city neighborhoods were likely to be desirable areas for investment and mortgage lending and which were to be avoided. The HOLC maps assigned neighborhoods into color-coded categories of desirability, with racial and ethnic composition a key factor. "Green" areas were deemed to have ideal conditions for investment, while "red" zones were "reserved for areas with dilapidated or informal housing stock and an 'undesirable population' of blacks, immigrants, and Jews." This is the origin of the term "redlining," used to describe the practice by government and private financial institutions of defining some areas as unworthy of investment.

These maps did not create the pattern of discriminatory investments in American cities, but they helped to facilitate it. A recent study of home mortgage lending and neighborhood investment in Philadelphia, for example, examined the lasting impact of the 1937 HOLC map of the city.[39] It found that even after adjusting for the racial composition and level of disadvantage present in various Philadelphia neighborhoods at that starting point, those census tracts that had been entirely within a "red zone" in 1937 had more than eight times the level of firearm assaults in 2013–14 as those that had been placed within a "green zone." In other words, "the same places that were imagined to be unworthy of economic investment by virtue of the races, ethnicities, and religions of the residents are more likely to be the places where violence and violent injury are most common almost a century later."[40]

This analysis drives home a crucial point: dangerous urban neighborhoods don't come from nowhere, and they are not the result of abstract, impersonal economic forces. They are products of what these researchers call "intergenerational social and economic exclusion." The patterns of deliberate, racially shaped disinvestment that the HOLC maps reflect were perfectly legal, and widely practiced, in the 1930s and 1940s. These practices are no longer legal—but as the studies make clear, they still operate in less formal ways, encouraging the concentration of minorities in areas that are systematically stripped of the private and public resources that people need to thrive.

IV

When you talk to people in these areas who are involved in violence, or likely to be, it is those things that they talk about the most: poverty, joblessness, uncertain futures, the anxieties of living in places that offer little support or personal protection other than what residents can provide for themselves, the emotional stresses and enduring scars caused by everyday racism. The quantitative studies we've just examined can seem very abstract, far removed from the real-world experience of the people whose lives are represented by a forbidding array of variables and equations. What's missing is the human meaning: how people actually make sense of their social environment and translate that understanding into action. But a tradition of on-the-ground qualitative research, stretching all the way back to Du Bois's work in the slums of late-nineteenth-century Philadelphia, gives us a rich sense of how these abstractions play out in real life.

Roughly a century after Du Bois first investigated the living conditions of Philadelphia's black population, for example, the sociologist Elijah Anderson, in his influential book *Code of the Street*, explored the personal and communal impact of joblessness and threadbare public supports in Philadelphia neighborhoods in the 1990s.[41] A key theme in Anderson's work is that though these neighborhoods suffer a great deal of violence, they are not monolithic. They are diverse places where some people manage reasonably well, others are "very poor but decent," and still others are "utterly and profoundly suffering, alienated, and angry."[42] There is a "basic tension" between the extremes of this distribution, between what Anderson calls "the street" and the "decent, more conventional world of legitimate jobs and stable families"—a "constant battle for the hearts and minds of the younger residents."[43] Especially in the most impoverished core of the city's African American neighborhoods, the "street" manifests itself as a distinct "oppositional culture" that is both a reaction to dire social and economic conditions and an important cause of their persistence, throwing up powerful barriers to youths' participation in "conventional" society.[44] Anderson's description of "street" culture is bleak: it reflects, he writes, an "acute alienation and social isolation from mainstream society and its institutions." Echoing Du Bois and the Blaus, he emphasizes that this alienation is a product of both material disadvantage and the awareness of racial injustice. It is not just that black street youth are faced with narrow and declining access to the "wider system of legitimate employment," but that they can "observe others—usually whites—enjoying the fruits of that system." In response, they develop "contempt for a society they perceive as having contempt for them."[45]

In this context, Anderson argues, violence has evolved over time to become a constant presence for nearly everyone, "decent" and "street" alike. It is a reality they must continually navigate, mainly through adopting what he calls the "code of the street"—a set of informal but essential guidelines for managing interpersonal encounters in this deeply fraught situation. Central to this code is the importance of respect, among people for whom getting respect in conventional ways has become more and more difficult. Where respect is in very short supply, Anderson argues, the "street" culture ratchets up its value in ways that maximize the potential for violence. "There is a general sense that very little respect is to be had, and therefore everyone competes to get what affirmation he can from what is available," he writes. "The resulting craving for respect gives people thin skins and short fuses."[46]

In this climate, what may seem from the outside to be stunningly trivial issues can become deadly conflicts. "You can get killed over one little simple hat," one of Anderson's informants says. "Like say I'm walking down the street and somebody try to take my hat from me and I won't let 'em take it and they got a gun."[47] The same need to maintain and preserve respect invites a dynamic of revenge and retaliation, which mandates "pay back" for attacks on you or your family.

The centrality of maintaining respect, to the point of being ready to injure or even kill someone who has crossed an arbitrary line, also represents a desperate attempt to obtain personal security in a world where the institutions that are, in theory, supposed to supply it are either incapable or unwilling to do so. In language that is remarkably similar to that of Du Bois, Dollard, and Myrdal, Anderson describes a local criminal justice system as "beset with a double standard: one for blacks and one for whites."[48] Ensuring real security for everyone is barely on its radar. "As the public authorities have seemingly abdicated their responsibilities," he writes, "many of those residing in such communities feel that they are on their own, that especially in matters of personal defense, they must assume the primary responsibility." "Abandoned is what you are," says one Philadelphia man quoted in *Code of the Street*,[49] and that bone-deep sense that you are on your own in a neglectful world is a key factor in the emergence of a street culture centered on the imperative of defending yourself with violence. In a world where the threat of violence is taken for granted, and where no one else can be depended on for help, doing violence well confers particular respect, even if—or especially if—it goes against the law.

As in Davis and Dollard's New Orleans of the 1930s, Anderson found that Philadelphia children in the 1990s learned early on "the first lesson of the streets: you cannot take survival itself, let alone respect, for granted; you have to fight for your place in the world." Many parents, he argues, strongly encourage retaliatory attitudes and the use of preemptive violence in their children, and "actually impose sanctions if a child is not sufficiently aggressive." A child who loses a fight might be told, "Don't you come in here crying that somebody beat you up; you better get back out there and whup his ass. . . . If you don't whup his ass, I'll whup yo' ass when you come home."[50]

Anderson has been criticized for seeming at times to suggest that it is mainly black youths' adherence to the "street" culture that now holds them back and keeps them from fully participating in "conventional" institutions like school and work, and that the burden is on black youth themselves to change their "outlook" on the world. "Simply providing opportunities is not enough," he insists in *Code of the Street*; young people "must also be encouraged to adopt an outlook that allows them to invest their considerable personal resources in available opportunities," and to "leave behind the attitudes, values, and behavior that work to block their advancement into the mainstream."[51] But this raises the question of how much it really makes sense to urge poor black youth to join the mainstream when the very idea of a "mainstream" has become problematic—when stability and economic security have retreated even for the children of what used to be the middle class. For many of the youth Anderson describes, arriving at a different "outlook" may in practice mean trying to adjust to a world of neglectful education, low-wage work, and diminished futures. That is a troubling implication, and in fact Anderson's language fits uneasily with his frequent advocacy for better jobs for inner-city youth. But his observations of contemporary Philadelphia descend in a straight line from earlier observers and support their core argument: inner-city violence is the product of a toxic mix of constricted opportunities and the abandonment of black communities by public institutions of security and support.

Similar themes appear again and again in qualitative work done in the roughly two decades since *Code of the Street* was written. They appear, for example, in a study by Joseph Richardson and his colleagues of young men convicted of violent crimes—mostly armed robbery—who were serving time in an urban jail in an unnamed large East Coast city. All of them—indeed, 100 percent of youth confined in the part of this jail reserved for juvenile offenders—were black; all of them lived in "impoverished neighborhoods with high rates of crime, violence, and unemployment."[52] Though they were all between fifteen and seventeen years old, their reading level ranged from fourth to eighth grade and some were "functionally illiterate." Indeed, tellingly, the researchers had planned to have the youths read books about gang violence in order to prepare for their focus groups but ended up using films instead because so many of them could not read.[53]

The level of violence these young men had experienced, both as victims and as perpetrators, was extraordinary. All of them said they had carried firearms "daily," all had witnessed a serious violent assault, and roughly three in four said they had personally witnessed a homicide. They took for granted that they would encounter violence regularly on the street and often described their own use of violence as "a form of labor." Living under conditions of chronic unemployment, and marginalized from opportunities and labor markets, they regarded economic crime in particular—including robbery, burglary, and drug dealing—as one of the few kinds of work realistically available to them. They routinely used the phrase "putting in work" to describe not only these economic crimes but other forms of personal violence that they engaged in as well. "Many youth in the study," the researchers wrote, "perceived building a reputation and acquiring and maintaining respect through the use of violence as a full-time occupation," and they worked "constantly" to "build and defend their reputations while simultaneously working to earn income from crime and violence." One young man they called "Dre" put it this way:

Nobody around our neighborhoods is working. So hitting someone's head [murder], it's like working. Younguns [adolescents] in my hood [neighborhood] already know they're not going to get no job and they're not going to college. So for them this is work: this is how they work.

He continued:

Bottom line, no matter what world you in, the underworld, the real world, whatever world, people want to be respected. In the underworld, the street world, you progress and get respect by putting in work [violence], doing things that other people in the real world might think is wrong, like laying somebody down [murder]. For us, hitting somebody's head [murder] might be the only way to deal with a situation. For some, it might bother you at first, you might have nightmares about it, but after you put in more work you get used to it. That's just how it is.[54]

Asked to rate the safety of their community on a scale from 1 to 10, with 10 being the most dangerous, one youth said: "I would rate it a 20. It's always somebody getting shot in my neighborhood." Every one of the respondents, according to the researchers, "expressed the need to carry a weapon at all times for protection." "I carry my gun anywhere I go," one seventeen-year-old said. "I mean if I got to crush [kill or maim] someone, then I will. I don't care. It's either him or me." Another revealed that he even carried his gun to the local mosque where he attended services on Friday afternoons. He acknowledged that he might be safe in the mosque itself, but "you still have to get back home."[55]

Richardson and his colleagues found that this dynamic was even more intense inside the jail than on the street. Young men behind bars felt that they had to be "hypervigilant," "always cognizant of the potential risk for violent victimization." But they also found that the jail system did little to help. Despite the extraordinary needs presented by the young men in this jail and other detention facilities for violent youth—including stunningly high levels of illiteracy and mental illness—the services available to them were typically minimal to nonexistent, rendering them thoroughly unprepared for their eventual return to "distressed communities where violence, crime, and infectious diseases are pervasive"[56] and accessible health and mental health care are scarce. And so the cycle of violence and response continues.

The researchers also found that these extremely violent incarcerated youth often developed a kind of numbness to the consequences of their actions, reflecting the desensitization we explored in chapter 2. They tended to believe that anyone who wound up as a victim probably had it coming. "We always say in my neighborhood, 'If you got did [murdered or violently assaulted] . . . then your ass deserved it!'" And they often displayed the sense of futurelessness we've already encountered. As one seventeen-year-old put it, "No matter what you do out here, you gonna die anyway; you can die stepping off a bus into the street. . . . I mean what's the difference? We all got to die."[57]

The criminologist Timothy Brezina and his colleagues found that the same mindset was central to the "existential" outlook of young men involved in street violence in Atlanta. A pervasive fatalism combined with a deeply pessimistic view of their chances of achieving a different kind of life bred a kind of "nihilism" in which not much mattered, even the likelihood of their own death. This meant, in effect, that anything was possible and indeed justifiable. "I say fuck tomorrow," one of their informants told them. "It's all about today. Might not be a tomorrow. Might get

shot. Might get hit by a bus. So get it now. Now, now, now.
Next week might as well be next century. Fuck next week.
Fuck tomorrow."[58]

The Atlanta researchers speculated that this attitude
facilitates violence in part by erasing young men's natural
fear of their own injury or death. But it seems also to involve
something more general, and even more troubling: what we
might call a "suspension of care," a shedding of concern for
the lives of others as well as oneself, in the context of a world
that is perceived as both unpredictable and without clearly
discernible meaning. They quote one seventeen-year-old to
this effect:

> My way of looking at this is, God gonna take everybody,
> okay? Gonna take me. Gonna take you. So, what the fuck
> am I gonna care for anybody? I'm not. I'm gonna get mine,
> and if I have to kill your ass to do it, so what? You'd kill
> me wouldn't you? Wouldn't you? So, what's the point?
> Might as well win. Somebody gotta win, somebody gotta
> lose. Gotta win until you lose. When you lose you dead.

Another young man says: "There's only a short time in the
world for everybody. I'm going to make yours shorter than
mine. Believe that. I don't think about nobody but me and
mines, you hear? No sympathy, no way."[59]

A young man the researchers call "Cris Cris" shows how
this worldview can breed a kind of reflexive and amoral
opportunism. "If I see something I want I take it right then
because that might be your only chance in this world to

get some. Somebody might be shootin' dice on the curb or something. I walk up and take all the money. So like that."[60] Intertwined with low "survival expectations," then, is something more profound: an acceptance of the world as a dog-eat-dog place where you can't depend on anyone but yourself. In the absence of more conventional skills and capacities, all you have to rely on is your ability to inspire fear—to be unambiguously "hard."

These studies focus on the responses of young people at the extreme—youth who are not just "at risk" of becoming involved in violence but already deeply enmeshed in it. But other studies of children and youth in impoverished black communities show that the sense of hopelessness and loss of meaning bred by endemic poverty, violence, and marginalization is not confined to a small "hard core."

In the 1990s, for example, Robert DuRant of Harvard Medical School and his colleagues interviewed children and youth, aged eleven to nineteen, in nine very poor public housing projects in Augusta, Georgia. The level of violence they found was extraordinary: 84 percent of the interviewees reported engaging in some kind of violent behavior. Fully one-quarter of the boys reported having been involved in a gang fight; more than a third said they had carried a weapon within the last thirty days, and one in five said they had attacked someone with a weapon "with the idea of seriously hurting or killing" them. A quarter of the girls, as well, said they had carried a weapon at some point, the majority of these within the last thirty days.

Even in these very poor projects, not all young people

had been involved in violence, much less serious violence. But those who were, DuRant found, had several things in common. One was having been the victim of violence in the past; another was what the researchers called "the hopelessness of social immobility." Youth who committed less violence, on the other hand, were more likely to feel that they had a purpose in life, and to expect to be "alive at age 25." These attitudes, in turn, were linked closely with whether their parents had work: children who lived in a household where the head was employed demonstrated less hopelessness, were more likely to believe that they would live to twenty-five, and scored higher on the measure of having a sense of purpose to their lives.[61]

The long-running study of youth in Mobile, Alabama, I mentioned in chapter 2 illustrates how deeply entrenched this syndrome of poverty, hopelessness, and violence remains, well into the era of the "crime decline." All told, between 1998 and 2006 the Mobile study involved more than seven thousand youth drawn from some of the most severely deprived parts of one of the most poverty-stricken urban areas in the country—neighborhoods where the average poverty rate was 57 percent and nearly a third of residents subsisted on less than half the poverty level. Focusing on a sample of more than seven hundred of these youth—aged ten to eighteen and more than 94 percent African American—the Mobile researchers found that, as in Augusta, striking numbers of them were involved in violence, often beginning at very young ages. But others were not, and which path they took was heavily influenced by what the researchers called "trajectories of hopelessness." Many children, of both genders, began adolescence with relatively low levels of hopelessness and stayed that way throughout. But others displayed an increasing sense of hopelessness over time, and it was among them that violence was the highest. Among the boys, *half* of those who were characterized as becoming increasingly hopeless over time had either threatened someone with a weapon in the past ninety days or actually shot or stabbed someone during the past year.

Surprisingly, the connection between hopelessness and violence weakened as the youth got older. During late adolescence, the proportion of boys who were involved in violence with a weapon was nearly the same among those who showed an increasing sense of hopelessness and those who reported *declining* levels of hopelessness. But the researchers suggested that this was not necessarily good news: it may have simply meant that the ever-present threat of violence around them bred a defensive violence among many boys from these neighborhoods, irrespective of what they thought about their futures. By that point, violence may have become less a response to a bleak outlook on the future than a practical strategy for defending themselves in an increasingly volatile world in the here and now.[62]

V

From W.E.B. Du Bois at the turn of the twentieth century to Kenneth Clark in the 1960s, the early students of the roots of violence in African American communities offered what at bottom were strikingly similar analyses of the source of the problem and strikingly similar warnings about what the future of these communities would look like in the absence of fundamental social change. Despite some differences in the settings they examined, the methods they employed, and the analytical tools they brought to bear, at the end of the day all of these observers wound up with the same essential message. Violence within the black community was a very real and often devastating problem. Contrary to common beliefs, it was not a reflection of anything innate about black people. Rather, it was a predictable response to conditions of life that were radically distinct from those of whites—and to their powerlessness to do much about them. And the implications for social action were also clear. Racial disparities in violence would be with us until and unless we addressed the deep inequalities that white America had created and enforced for generations.

Another half century of research has not seriously challenged that analysis or shaken those implications. It shows that contemporary black communities' struggles with violence are a direct reflection of generations of economic and social disadvantages that remain largely unaddressed. There are differences of emphasis among various studies, and there are controversies about the precise mechanisms that link racial inequality to violence. But there is no real dispute about the bigger picture. Violence flourishes in communities where many people have been stripped of the social supports and opportunities that they need to thrive and where expectations of personal security and a meaningful future have been systematically thwarted or stillborn. In a society distinctive for its generally heedless and neglectful social policies, those conditions have affected some people of every race. But enduring discrimination has made African Americans especially vulnerable. Nothing short of restoring those stolen opportunities and depleted supports will suffice to eliminate the long-standing racial inequalities of life and death. In the next chapter, I want to explore what that might mean in practice.

FIVE

REMEDIES

More than a century after W.E.B. Du Bois moved into Philadelphia's troubled Seventh Ward, murder still "sits at the doorsteps" in all too many African American communities. Of all the stubbornly enduring racial inequalities in our society, the racial divide in the experience of violence is one of the most profound and consequential.

The most urgent remedies flow naturally from the analysis of the causes. We've seen that the endemic violence in many black communities reflects the extraordinary levels of deprivation, insecurity, and thwarted opportunity they continue to face even in times of great wealth and strong economic growth in the society as a whole. Those problems are deepened by the ongoing legacy of racial segregation and by a system of social control that itself too often adds to the danger African Americans face rather than protecting them from it. Violence is bred by the continuing presence of living conditions that, at the extreme, more closely resemble those in much poorer countries than in the rest of the developed world and are so far removed from those of most whites that it is difficult even to compare them. It should go without saying that not all black communities in the United States share those deprived conditions, and that even those that do possess impressive reservoirs of energy, commitment, and skills. But in the midst of unprecedented national wealth and technological capacity, too many Americans still suffer from a toxic mix of adversities that includes extreme poverty, desperately inadequate schools and public services, inaccessible and inferior health care, and an ongoing crisis of joblessness and youth disconnection that is disturbingly resistant to economic growth. Their communities can justifiably be described as abandoned, and that abandonment has worsened, in some ways, in the current social and political climate.

There are, to be sure, some things we could do—and are doing—to reduce violence without directly addressing that abandonment. But, with some exceptions that we'll consider in a moment, those alternatives cannot by themselves take us very far. Keep in mind that we have already tried some of them. We have tried to deal with this massive public health crisis through small-scale, underfunded programs. We have tried to deal with it through vastly increased punishment and surveillance—one of the most thoroughly implemented experiments in social engineering in living memory. But people keep on dying.

In this chapter, I want to talk about some of the things that might make a real difference. This is not an exhaustive list of every program and every policy that shows some promise in helping to reduce violence. Many approaches have been found to be modestly effective, at least in the short term, and I will mention some of them here. But if we have learned one thing from decades of experience, it is that even well-conceived initiatives, unless they are linked to more fundamental changes, ultimately will be thwarted by the overarching environment of systemic neglect and racialized inequality. It's crucial to recognize that the main reason other communities—and other countries—suffer less violence is not because they have more or better programs for people at high risk but because they have fewer people at high risk in the first place. So I want to focus here on some key strategies to address the roots of violence that emerge from the accumulated research. Most of these are not altogether new: they are variations on remedies that careful observers have been urging for a long time.

I

The cornerstone of any serious effort to reduce the burden of endemic violence must be a guarantee of meaningful employment for everyone able to work, at wages that can support a decent standard of living. Doing this is crucial for two related reasons. First, good jobs themselves directly attack the marginalization, deprivation, hopelessness, and insecurity from which violence grows. Second, a full-employment strategy can also provide the human resources that will enable us to address the other fundamental adversities that are routinely associated with racial disparities in violence: neglected schools, inadequate health and mental health care, a reactive and counterproductive criminal justice system, and much more. It is therefore the single most critical element in a strategy to build the thriving communities of support and opportunity that are the best defense against violence in the long run.

In the United States as a whole, the overall black rate of unemployment is currently about twice that of whites. In some states it is even higher than that: as 2019 began it was triple the white rate in Alabama and close to that in Mississippi.[1] That gap persists in spite of the considerable economic growth since the Great Recession: in the past decade unemployment rates have fallen for all racial and ethnic groups, and indeed faster for African Americans than anyone else. The fact that the overall black unemployment rate remained double that of whites in 2019 tells us that economic growth alone is not enough to close the gap. (The economic crisis created by the policy response to the coronavirus pandemic in 2020, moreover, has put an end to this period of declining unemployment, at least for a while.) And the disconnect between economic growth and the availability of good work is most pronounced among black youth. In 2017, when the economy had been expanding for several years, nearly a quarter of black high school *graduates* aged eighteen to twenty-one who were not enrolled in further schooling were officially unemployed. That was lower than the rate at the height of the recession, but it was still higher than at the start of the twenty-first century—and roughly twice the rate for white high school graduates.[2]

What's more, the US Department of Labor only considers people as "unemployed" if they are not only jobless but have actively looked for work in the past four weeks. The official unemployment figures therefore notoriously understate the depth of the job problem, since they leave out those who have given up on finding employment and are out of the labor force altogether—or who still want a job but, for one reason or another, have not looked for one in the past month. More comprehensive measures of joblessness give a fuller picture, particularly when we look at the places where the problem is most concentrated. In Chicago, for example, according to a report from the Great Cities Initiative of the University of Illinois at Chicago, slightly more than *half* of black men aged twenty to twenty-four were out of work in 2016 (where "out of work" was defined to include both the officially unemployed and those out of the labor force). That was more than twice the proportion of non-Hispanic white men that age.[3]

An even more troubling number tracked by the Great Cities Initiative is the proportion of youth who are "disconnected from work and civic life," meaning that they neither have a job nor are enrolled in school.[4] Nationwide, almost a million young black men and women, ages sixteen to twenty-four, were "disconnected" by this definition in 2017.[5] In Chicago, among black men ages twenty to twenty-four, the disconnected rate reached 45 percent—six times the rate among white men of that age and more than twice the rate for Latinos. In that city alone, therefore, nearly thirteen thousand black men aged twenty to twenty-four were neither in school nor at work. Young black women in Chicago fared almost as badly: over 30 percent of them were disconnected from school and work in 2017, more than seven times the proportion among their white counterparts.[6] In some Illinois counties from 2012 to 2016, the proportion of black youth of both sexes out of school and out of work topped 60 percent.[7]

The Great Cities reports also point to another critical part of the job problem: not only are startling numbers of young people, particularly young minority men, out of work altogether, but many of those who do have work are in the low-wage jobs that have accounted for most of the recent employment growth in the state.[8] The problem is compounded by the fact that increasing numbers of youth are able to find only part-time jobs, making it hard to obtain anything approaching economic security. A recent report by the Economic Policy Institute demonstrates this on the national level. Almost 28 percent of young black high school graduates who are not enrolled in further schooling, it shows, are "underemployed"—which includes not only the officially unemployed but also those working only part-time when they want full-time jobs and those who have looked for work within the past year but not within the last few weeks. Measured this way, underemployment among both Latinos and non-Hispanic whites is bad enough—18 percent to 19 percent of them are underemployed by this definition—but they do not approach the rate for African Americans.[9] And these are high school *graduates*. By all measures, the deficit of good work is worse—sometimes far worse—for black youth without a high school degree.

The stubbornness of underemployment even after years of post-recession economic growth confirms Gunnar Myrdal's insight from more than half a century ago: simply stimulating the private economy isn't enough. Seriously tackling the high levels of joblessness and underemployment among African Americans requires directing public resources into job creation and training, guided by thoughtful planning to ensure that the jobs we create are useful and that the money we invest in them is well spent. There have been several proposals in the last few years to do just that.

Some economists have proposed what they call a "job guarantee" as a response both to the unemployment caused by the routine ups and downs of the economy and the chronic, endemic joblessness that afflicts some people and places even in good times. Mark Paul, William Darity Jr., and Darrick Hamilton of Duke University, for example, have called for the creation of a National Investment Employment Corps that would provide publicly subsidized work for "all persons seeking a job." The program would be administered by the US Department of Labor, which would provide funds to states or local governments to develop employment projects "designed to address community needs and provide socially beneficial goods and services to communities and society at large."[10] Paul, Darity, and Hamilton emphasize jobs designed to enhance the country's infrastructure—upgrading public and private buildings, restoring the environment, developing energy strategies to reduce the country's carbon footprint—but they also stress the need for new jobs in high-quality pre-school and after-school programs, eldercare, and other crucial but now badly underfunded and understaffed social services. They point to other possibilities as well, including "rejuvenation of the nation's defunded Postal Service," support for the arts, and much more. Anyone over the age of eighteen would be eligible for the program, whether they were officially unemployed, underemployed, or outside the labor force. The jobs could be either full-time or part-time; they would come with benefits and what the proposal calls a "non-poverty" wage—defined as a little under $12 an hour in 2018—which would be indexed to inflation.

Paul, Darity, and Hamilton acknowledge that guaranteeing jobs that pay wages above the poverty level would not be cheap, at least at first. They estimate that funding this strategy on a level sufficient to address the rate of unemployment and underemployment at the start of 2018 would have cost roughly $543 billion.[11] But they point out that these costs would be substantially offset by the economic benefits that would flow from universal full employment. Putting more people to work at decent wages would bring substantial increases in tax revenues. And it would reduce spending on income support and social insurance programs, since many more people would become self-sufficient. Spending on unemployment insurance would fall; so would spending on the Temporary Assistance for Needy Families (TANF) program—"welfare"—because there would be far fewer "needy" families to assist. Likewise, one of the biggest up-front costs of a job guarantee would be the expense of giving health benefits to new workers, but providing those through the job program itself would reduce the amount we spend through existing health programs—notably the national Medicaid program for low-income people, which cost $368 billion in 2016.

And we could expect other kinds of savings as well. As Myrdal and others explained as far back as the early 1960s, mass long-term joblessness, in addition to being deeply damaging to individuals and the communities they live in, is also economically wasteful because it erodes productive capacity. People who are out of work for a long time often lose whatever skills they have learned, and those who are unable to get a good job to begin with never develop them in the first place, which drags down economic output. Reversing that process—building skills and putting them to use rather than enforcing idleness—pays for itself over time. And as Paul, Darity, and Hamilton point out, the kinds of strategic investments the job guarantee would support—in infrastructure, early education and childcare services, and environmental remediation, among others— would themselves contribute enormously to the productivity of the economy as a whole.

Over the long term, then, giving people jobs, while it requires a substantial outlay to begin with, is far better for the health of the economy than keeping them out of work or leaving them employed at such low wages that they are unable to thrive. And because of the truly universal character of the job guarantee, we could also employ a great many people who are jobless today not because they don't want to work but because the private job market often doesn't want them—including many people with physical or social disabilities who have real contributions to make but are typically shunned by the conventional labor market.

Some economists worry that setting up a large-scale public job creation program that swells and contracts with the ups and downs of the economy would present formidable practical problems—that the complexities of putting in place enough jobs to accommodate everyone left jobless in recessions, for example, and then releasing them back into "regular" jobs when the economy picks up, would require a much greater managerial capacity than the country now possesses.[12] And that's an important concern. But rather than undermining the case for public investment toward full employment, what this suggests is that it may be better to think of public job creation as a permanent strategy targeted at rebuilding our depleted public institutions rather than a temporary stopgap to provide jobs when the private economy isn't working well.

The erosion of those public institutions—from schools to housing to social services—has had a devastating impact on low-income communities in general and on African American communities in particular. Compared with other advanced industrial countries, the United States has always underfunded its essential public sector, and that perennial problem has grown in an era of ascendant anti-government ideology and crippling cuts in domestic public spending. The accumulated impact has been catastrophic in some places, and nowhere more than in the deeply impoverished communities where violence is worst. So, as I've suggested, there is an opportunity here to accomplish two hugely beneficial things at once. Fully funding our public schools, health-care systems, and other crucial institutions can put large numbers of people to work in socially useful tasks at living wages and at the same time can go a long way toward restoring the essential public functions on which healthy and secure communities depend.

Consider the schools. One of the defining features of public education in America, in contrast to many other advanced industrial societies, is that the quality of public education varies dramatically among communities with different social and economic resources. Nationally, funding for school personnel has steadily eroded for decades—one result of what a coalition of school advocates in Los Angeles describes as a policy of "manufactured austerity" that has created school systems that are "broke on purpose."[13] The problem worsened dramatically during the recession that began in 2008, and though things have improved since then, staffing levels in public schools, particularly in the most resource-deprived urban and rural areas, have never recovered. In 2018, the number of school personnel— including teachers, librarians, nurses, and other staff—was down by more than 150,000 from 2008, while the number of children enrolled in the public schools had *increased* by roughly 1.4 million over that period. Since school staffing was already inadequate to meet the need before the recession, the Center on Budget and Policy Priorities estimates that as of 2018, the United States faced a shortfall of at least 300,000 school personnel across the country.[14] And those national figures mask the shortfall's concentration in schools that already have the fewest resources. Better-off school districts can often make up deficits in state and federal funding, either by drawing on a more robust local tax base or raising private funds from their more affluent constituents; poorer ones don't have those options. And since the poorer schools typically confront a much deeper—and more expensive—set of issues among their students, they feel the impact of shrinking budgets even more heavily.

In Detroit, where youth violence perennially reaches levels that are among the highest in the United States (and the world), public school classes can run up to forty-five to fifty students per teacher, which likely has something to do with why the city's schools ranked last in the country among urban school districts in fourth- and eighth-grade achievement for several years running.[15] In Flint, a recent community protest highlighted the fact that at least thirteen classes at a local high school had been without a teacher at all for three months.[16] In Illinois, just 700 school nurses, many of them working part-time, serve a total of 3,796 public schools—at a time when school nurses are called upon to take on a much bigger load than in the past, especially in poor communities, where budget cuts in outside mental health services for children have forced nurses into the front lines of mental health care.[17]

A real commitment to investing in funding for public school jobs—for nurses, teachers, special education staff, classroom aides, and other personnel now in short supply— could turn this crisis into an opportunity. It would allow us to build a rich school culture of nurturance and support in communities that have been progressively stripped of adult resources. Turning what are now neglected and sometimes nearly abandoned schools into places where a community of competent, caring, and well-rewarded adults can reliably guide, mentor, and nurture children would strike at the root of two critical problems—joblessness and the systemic neglect of poor children—at the same time. A commitment to full employment backed by a job guarantee could also help provide the workforce for the nearly $200 billion worth of deferred structural repairs that schools across the country desperately need—a deficit that subjects poor children to everything from toxic chemical exposures to freezing classrooms to rodents in the hallways.[18] Fixing such problems requires stable funding, and a job guarantee at the national level can go a long way toward overcoming the limits and uncertainties of local school budgets.

The years before school hold similar potential. As a recent report from the Center on Budget and Policy Priorities points out, our current national spending on childcare and early education ranks us roughly on the level of countries like Estonia and Turkey; New Zealand, France, and the Nordic countries spend at least twice the proportion of their national product on early care as we do. The result is a system that fails both the children and parents it is supposed to serve and the workers—disproportionately workers of color—whose low-wage labor in effect subsidizes it in the absence of sufficient public funding. The CBPP report estimates that California alone will need several hundred thousand childcare and early education workers in the coming years; a full-employment policy geared to sustaining and enhancing vital public institutions could provide them.[19]

Our broken health-care system offers another opportunity. As with schooling, the United States is distinct from other advanced industrial societies in the degree to which access to adequate health care is dependent on personal economic resources. In practice, what this means is that many of the communities where the need for high-quality health care is greatest are also the places least likely to get it. We know that this has multiple adverse effects on virtually every dimension of health for poor Americans, from heart disease to diabetes, from drug abuse and dental problems to maternal mortality and HIV. Those health deficits, in turn, translate into increased risks of poverty and underemployment, adding to the overall burden of economic deprivation and insecurity. Part of the problem is the perennial shortage of health-care workers, especially in the public sector, who can be deployed to the poorest and most underserved communities—some of which now amount to "medical deserts." This means that many low-income people cannot find basic medical care even when they could, in theory, afford it—a problem exacerbated by the recent refusal of some states to take advantage of federal funds available to expand the Medicaid program. Building the health-care workforce through a job guarantee coupled with appropriate training could provide large numbers of good, meaningful, and permanent jobs and simultaneously help build a vibrant and accessible public health-care sector offering critical services to the communities in need. And many of those health services, including well-designed substance abuse treatment and mental health programs, can themselves directly help to reduce the potential for violence.

These needs are already great, and they will grow. One recent report estimates that the United States will need over 2.3 million new health workers by 2025, a gap driven especially by the health needs of an aging population. That includes more than 400,000 home health-care workers, nearly 100,000 medical and laboratory technicians, and 95,000 nursing assistants, as well as close to a million nurses.[20] And the need will be especially critical in the places that are now most underserved. The private labor market has proven incapable of keeping up with this demand. It is encouraging that serious proposals for a universal health-care system are now at the center of national political dialogue in the United States. But if we do create the kind of universal system that can finally bring the United States into the ranks of advanced societies that cover all of their people against the risks and ravages of illness, we will need many more doctors, nurses, and medical technicians to staff it.

The urgency of the need for greater public investment

in our health-care workforce was put in stark relief by the onslaught of the COVID-19 pandemic in 2020. Just the year before, the nonprofit Trust for America's Health estimated that the country's public health efforts were roughly $4.5 billion below their proper budget levels, leaving state and local governments "woefully underfunded to address public health emergencies such as infectious disease outbreaks, extreme weather events, and the opioid crisis."[21] From 2001 to 2018, funding to "support and maintain state and local public health preparedness" had been cut by about 28 percent, and funding specifically designated for "health care emergency preparedness" had been slashed by nearly half.[22] Local health departments lost an estimated fifty-eight thousand workers during the post-2008 recession, and unlike other kinds of public employment, those jobs did not "rebound" afterward. Public health agencies, as a result, were "fraught with high staff turnover due to burnout from heavy workloads and low staffing levels."[23] It hardly needs saying that building up our capacity to provide effective prevention, testing, and treatment is critical today and will continue to be in the future. And it would also bring the promise of important and rewarding work for tens of thousands of Americans in need of it.

In short, one of the great benefits of guaranteeing meaningful work for everyone is that it would allow us to do a much better job of providing social goods that we need anyway. Whether we are talking about helping at-risk youth, supplying more and better-trained childcare workers, teachers, and medical personnel, or giving people the skills to restore a functioning infrastructure, we are not talking about providing just any job, much less wasteful "make-work." We are seeing to it that our people are engaged in work that offers meaning and purpose as well as a solid living, and, at the same time, that those who most need our help are finally able to get it. And on both counts, the people who stand to benefit the most from that commitment will be those who have been historically the most excluded both from rewarding work and from social supports.

II

Providing useful and permanent jobs—and thereby dramatically transforming what criminologists have often called the "opportunity structure"—would also essentially eliminate a major problem that has bedeviled the short-term work programs that have been a mainstay of our halting efforts to expand opportunities for vulnerable Americans. Research shows that when they are done well such programs can work even for very troubled populations—but only up to a point. Even well-designed and well-run programs are often stymied by the absence of good permanent jobs in the larger economy. Evaluations of the federal Job Corps and smaller-scale initiatives around the country thus often show a revealing pattern. There are reductions in crime or drug abuse while participants are *in* the program—but the gains fade or wash out entirely once they leave the artificial conditions of the program itself and venture into the "regular" labor market.[24] This frustrating outcome doesn't tell us that these programs don't work; what it tells us is that the "regular" labor market can't, on its own, fulfill the promise that good work offers as a strategy to reduce violence.

And that promise is very real. Some evidence comes from a program called One Summer Chicago Plus, which provides jobs during the summer for youth from some of Chicago's most troubled neighborhoods.[25] In the summer of 2012, the program, run by the city's Department of Family and Support Services, enrolled about seven hundred youth, ages fourteen to twenty-one, from "high-violence high schools" in an eight-week job program. They worked in government and nonprofit agencies, at minimum wage, for about twenty-five hours a week, and had a day of training in "job readiness"; some also spent a couple of hours a day in what the program called a "social emotional learning curriculum." The following year, the strategy changed somewhat in order to increase participation from the youth at greatest risk: this time the participants were all male, from sixteen to twenty-two years old, and were recruited from criminal justice agencies as well as from high-violence neighborhoods. Another change was that the 2013 summer program ran for six weeks rather than eight. In both years, far more youth wanted to join the program than could be accommodated, so they were selected by lottery—which also enabled researchers to compare young people with similar characteristics and from similar neighborhoods who either got into the program through the lottery or did not.

The results were striking. Arrests for violent crime

among participants in the One Summer Chicago Plus program in 2012 were estimated to be 42 percent lower than those of similar youth who had applied to the program but not gotten into it. In 2013, with a somewhat more difficult population and a shorter program, the decline in violent arrests was still an estimated 33 percent. In absolute terms, that meant that roughly one in four of the control group, who had *not* participated in the program, were arrested during the first year after they applied, versus about one in six of those who had participated. One in six is still a very high number—but it is also a lot better than one in four. And these differences are all the more remarkable because the jobs lasted only a few weeks.

But some important limitations also come through in the program evaluation. The researchers found that, as in previous short-term job programs, the differences in arrests began to fade out over time, though they did not disappear completely. After two to three years, those who participated in the program had about 20 percent fewer violent arrests than those who did not. Notably, the researchers also found that the program by itself did not significantly improve the participants' chances of working in the formal labor market after they left. And the evaluation also turned up another pattern that is disturbingly familiar in programs like these: One Summer Chicago Plus seemed to work best for participants who were less troubled and less deprived—and not as well for those at the highest risk of violence. As the researchers put it, the youth who benefited the most from the program were "younger, more school-engaged, less likely to have been arrested, more likely to be Hispanic, and living in neighborhoods with slightly lower unemployment rates. In other words, they are not the out-of-school, out-of-work youth typically served by youth employment programs."[26] The researchers concluded that, overall, the news about this program was good, particularly because summer job programs are relatively inexpensive and can thus become "a powerful, accessible tool for cities seeking to shift outcomes and improve lives."[27] That's true, but an even more important takeaway point is what this program suggests might be possible with a bigger effort. If we can accomplish significant change in a six-week program offering minimum-wage jobs, we would surely be able to accomplish more, in more enduring ways, through a comprehensive full-employment program that can provide permanent positions in meaningful work oriented toward social needs—long-term jobs with a future that young people can look forward to as they grow up.

A full-fledged commitment to public investment could also provide the greatly expanded system of job training we will need in a twenty-first-century society. The American economy today presents a paradoxical combination of, on one hand, stubborn, concentrated joblessness for some people and places, and, on the other, a shortage of capable workers to fill higher-skill jobs. Our approach to the labor market thus fails in two directions at once: it does not reliably provide enough good jobs to meet the need, even in times of prosperity, and it does not consistently supply qualified workers to fill the good jobs we do create. Both failures reflect the same overarching problem: as Gunnar Myrdal and many other observers lamented as far back as the 1940s, we leave this most crucial of social outcomes— whether or not our people can earn a livelihood—mostly up to the uncertain fortunes of the private labor market, and do very little by way of consciously designing an employment policy that meets both human and economic needs. Publicly funded job creation is one part of a more mindful approach of this kind; another is public investment in programs that train people in necessary skills and link them with real jobs in both the private and public sectors.

Many countries—notably including Germany, Denmark, and Switzerland, which not coincidentally boast very low levels of youth violence—accomplish this through extensive apprenticeship programs, which combine on-the-job training with classroom education and a commitment by employers to provide a permanent job when the training is completed. In Switzerland, 40 percent of employers participate in these programs, and roughly two out of three young people enter the world of work through an apprenticeship.[28] Once mainly focused on blue-collar trades—electrical work, plumbing, baking, and the like— apprenticeships are increasingly found across the spectrum of occupations, from banking to cybersecurity. The comparatively small number of apprenticeship programs in the United States grew significantly during the Obama administration, which recognized their potential both as engines of productivity and as a strategy to combat youth disconnection and underemployment. But we still lag far behind many other countries, and a big part of the reason is that in the absence of a commitment to invest public resources in these programs, most of the up-front cost—which can be considerable—falls on private employers, and to a lesser extent on students and their families.

If we've learned anything from our dismal history of concentrated joblessness, it is that making the fullest use of young people's potential won't happen automatically, as a happy by-product of the haphazard operation of the private labor market. The wishful fantasy that the market will suffice has given us a "system" that leaves great numbers of young people—even those with a high school education and beyond—to flounder without a reliable connection to sustaining and purposeful work, while simultaneously depriving the economy of the contributions they could make if we gave them a chance, and meanwhile saddling taxpayers with massive expenditures to pick up the pieces. There is plenty of room for argument about how best to deliver public investment in job training; what's crucial, again, is to commit ourselves to the principle.

One promising example is the CareerWise Colorado program, launched in 2017 as a pilot project that aims ultimately to enroll twenty thousand young people statewide, or roughly 10 percent of the state's high school students. The program, which draws from the Swiss experience with apprenticeship training, links students with specific employers—in fields ranging from advanced manufacturing to information technology to financial services—in a curriculum that blends regular school courses with serious on-the-job training in an actual workplace. It's a new program, and it's too soon to tell how effective it will be. But it is a big step in the right direction, and the most ambitious effort of its kind we've seen so far in the United States.[29]

III

Guaranteeing good work with reasonable wages, and the training to make it feasible, would also strike a powerful blow against the extreme and intractable poverty that, as we've seen, is so closely linked to endemic violence. People are poor in the United States in large part because they have either no work or poorly paid work; and long-term joblessness in particular helps trap people in the kind of chronic poverty that typically afflicts the most violent communities in America. Close to half of poor people who are employed full-time, according to the US Census Bureau, manage to escape poverty after three years; only about a third of those who are without work do so. Overall, the rate of poverty among people who do not work at all over the course of a year is more than ten times that of those who work full-time and year-round.[30]

But American poverty, especially among minorities, is also about low pay (which is why millions of employed people still can't escape it), and there is no more powerful weapon against poverty-level wages than a full-employment policy with a job guarantee. That so many of the jobs we have recently gained, even in a period of substantial economic growth, pay wages that are too low to provide a decent living is particularly troubling because we know that low-wage work makes its own distinctive contributions to violence. Parents trapped in low-paying work, for example, are often forced to juggle two or even three jobs, leaving them unavailable to their children. And the prospect of a future of uninspiring, low-wage, dead-end jobs can't effectively compete with the appeal of illicit work or provide the sense of meaning and purpose that may be the most reliable defense against violence.

Working people of every race, of course, are affected by poverty-level wages. But low wages are much more common among black and Hispanic workers than among whites, and the gap remains basically unchanged in spite of recent improvements in the economy as a whole. In 2017, according to the Economic Policy Institute, about one in seven black workers in the United States—versus about one in eleven whites—was paid hourly wages that, even if they worked full-time and year-round, would leave them below the poverty line if they were the sole earner in their family. And that disparity has persisted, mostly unchanged, since at least the mid-1980s.[31]

We often associate the growth of low-wage work with the decline of better-paid manufacturing jobs, and that's certainly part of the problem. But another part is the precipitous decline of employment in the public sector, which has traditionally been one of the most reliable avenues into the ranks of the middle class, especially for blacks and other minorities. The relentless chipping away of public-sector employment in recent years has been a kind of stealth disaster for the black community, and one whose full consequences may not be felt until much further down the road. This is all the more reason why it's imperative to invest in rebuilding a strong public sector in the United States. But as it stands, we are moving backward in this respect—recently, at breakneck speed. Severe and continuing budget cuts at the federal and state levels, in tandem with Supreme Court decisions restricting the ability of organized labor to bargain for public workers, represent an ongoing assault on the well-being and security of a wide swath of middle-income minority workers.

As an Economic Policy Institute report puts it, state and local workers have been "hammered by years of austerity policy at all levels of government." This attack on public-sector workers "not only lessens those workers' ability to make ends meet, but undermines the public services they provide."[32] In a survey of childcare and early education teaching staff in New York, for example, researchers found that 71 percent "worried about paying housing costs," 70 percent worried that they would not be able to pay for routine health care, and fully half "worried about having enough food for their families."[33] Again, the private labor market has not much eased this burden, but a full-employment guarantee, with a focus on providing critical social services and fairly paying the people who deliver them, could.

The second reason why the United States remains an outlier when it comes to poverty in general, and extreme poverty in particular, is that our income supports for people who do *not* have jobs are pitched so low. That is hardly an accident: social benefits have deliberately been kept low, especially for blacks and other minorities, in order to enforce low-wage work—a practice that is deeply rooted in the economic history of the Jim Crow South. The problem has been intensified in recent years by the promotion of austerity policies by both political parties, and by a relentless ideology that denigrates public spending, especially spending to help the poor. One of the most beneficial impacts of a full-employment policy is that it would also make it feasible to provide more generous support for those who cannot work, whether temporarily or permanently—in part because there would be fewer people who need that support, but also because higher wages overall would mean that it's possible to give more generous benefits to those who can't work without those benefits being seen as a disincentive for people to get a job.

My emphasis on poverty reduction as a key strategy against violence may strike some people as impractical. But the pessimistic view that we can't do much about the deep poverty that has crippled so many American communities of all races is trumped by real-world evidence. The United States' overall levels of poverty even in good times tower above those of most of our advanced industrial counterparts around the globe. Even after several years of generally strong economic growth, more than one in every six

American children—and nearly three out of ten African American children—live below the federal poverty level. It is the highest child poverty rate in the advanced industrial world. At the other extreme, countries like Denmark and Finland have driven child poverty rates below 4 percent. Most of the world's other advanced industrial nations fall in between, but generally much closer to Denmark than to the United States.[34] One very important reason for these disparities—which, barring a significant redirection of our social and economic policies, will not go away—is that those countries spend a much larger proportion of their national resources on providing income support to vulnerable children and families, and accordingly do much better at protecting the well-being of people who are not well served by market forces. Our atypical level of child poverty is not inevitable, and it is not the result of neutral economic or technological factors. We are as rich as (indeed, most often richer than) many countries that have done a far better job of reducing poverty among children. The reasons for these disparities are entirely political—the result, again, of choices we have made and choices we have failed to make.

And make no mistake, the effect on violence of a significant reduction in severe poverty would be very substantial. A recent study by Heather Sipsma of the Yale School of Public Health and her colleagues helps to put this in quantitative perspective. They studied the variation in spending on the poor across forty-one states and the District of Columbia, and matched states' level of spending with their average homicide rates for the years 2005 through 2009.

They found that with all else controlled, every $10,000 increase in spending per person living in poverty translated into a roughly 16 percent decrease in the average homicide rate—which, on the national level, equals more than twenty-six hundred fewer homicides each year.[35]

IV

A full-on commitment to full employment would have another benefit, as well: it could help transform our swollen and counterproductive criminal punishment system. It's no secret that our main response as a society to high levels of violence in the African American community, at least since the early 1970s, has been to put far more people behind bars and increase the sentences they must serve.[36] There is by now a widespread consensus—one that to some extent transcends political divisions—that as a strategy to ensure public safety this has been a dramatic failure, and a mind-bogglingly costly one; and that it has had a shockingly disparate impact on communities of color.[37] What's less often recognized are the ways in which our decades-long commitment to this failed strategy has itself contributed to the problem it was ostensibly designed to solve. The early writers on race and crime, as we've seen, were united in believing that a caste system of justice could itself breed violence—both by stoking a corrosive sense of injustice and alienation and by failing to protect black Americans from communal violence. But they could have had no inkling of the transformation of criminal punishment that was to come after the 1960s.

One telling indication of how deeply things have changed in the past half century is that the massively detailed Kerner Commission report on the roots of urban disorders, published in 1968, has no index entry for "prisons" or "prison system."[38] The looming presence of the prison in the life of many black American communities today has been thoroughly charted, so I will only briefly mention some of the dimensions of the change that has taken place over the last several decades. In 1978, there were roughly 143,000 black Americans in all state and federal prisons combined. By the end of 2017, more than that many were incarcerated in just three states—California, Florida, and Texas—alone.[39] At the high point of African American incarceration in the United States, in 2007, there were 593,000 black Americans in prison. Since then, the number has declined by nearly 20 percent, but more than 475,000 remain in prison across the country. The prison incarceration rate for African American men is more than 2,300 per 100,000 population, six times the rate for whites. Among black men aged thirty-five to thirty-nine—the group most likely to be in a state or federal prison—the imprisonment rate in 2017 was well over 5,200 per 100,000, meaning that one in every nineteen black men that age was in prison, versus fewer than one in a hundred whites. Startlingly, mirroring the pattern of the racial gap in homicide death rates, the imprisonment rate among older black men, aged sixty to sixty-four, is considerably higher than the *highest* rate among young white men.[40] These figures, moreover, do not count men locked in local jails, and they count only those incarcerated at one particular moment—not the far larger number who "flow" in and out of jails and prisons over time. And, again as with homicide rates, the full import of the high black incarceration rate in America is partly masked in these comparative statistics because the rates for non-Hispanic whites in the United States are themselves quite high by the standards of the rest of the advanced industrial world. At nearly 400 per 100,000 in 2017, the incarceration rate for white men in America was higher than the overall male imprisonment rate in the United Kingdom—itself the highest in Western Europe.[41]

The persistence of endemic violence in the face of unprecedented levels of incarceration is powerful evidence that even massive investments in fear and incapacitation do not reliably counter the social forces that breed it. But the figures also point to another and even more disturbing reality: in many ways, that investment has made the problem worse. This is partly because mass incarceration has led to disabling consequences for former prisoners—and we now have an extensive body of research illuminating the multiple ways in which it increases already formidable barriers in access to jobs, housing, social services, education, and more. We know, too, that mass incarceration has often undercut normal family life and eroded the capacity of already strained communities to nurture and guide the young.[42]

A dysfunctional, punitive, and reactive criminal justice system, moreover, helps to breed violence not only by what it does to people but by what it does *not* do—not only through the ways in which it actively harms people, but through what it passively fails to do for them. One telling indication of this comes from studies concluding that being involved in the criminal justice system is associated with an increased likelihood of becoming a victim of violence afterward. Linda Teplin and her colleagues at Northwestern University's School of Medicine, for example, conducted a study of roughly eighteen hundred youth sent to a juvenile detention center in Chicago, following them on average for seven years after their admission to the facility. During that time, sixty-five of the youth died—and of these, 90 percent were victims of homicide and another 5 percent of "legal intervention" (that is, they were killed by police). Male African American youth, not surprisingly, had the highest death rate, which was four times the already very high death rate of black male youth in the community in general.[43]

A more recent study by a team of researchers from the Indiana University School of Medicine adds another dimension to this analysis, showing that the more deeply youth are pulled into the justice system, the more likely they are to die prematurely after they leave. Among nearly fifty thousand Indianapolis youth who were arrested and referred to juvenile court from 1999 to 2011, those who were detained in a juvenile facility for a short term were about twice as likely to die as those who had only been arrested; those sent to a youth prison for a longer term, two and a half times as likely; and those transferred to adult court—the most serious disposition—more than three and a half times as likely. That pattern closely paralleled the racial distribution of youth across the different dispositions. Blacks were 28 percent of the county's youth overall but were 48 percent of those arrested, 52 percent of those detained for a short term, 58 percent of those incarcerated in youth prison, and 69 percent of those sent to adult court. The researchers conclude with the stark assessment that "the greater the extent of an individual's justice system involvement, the greater the risk of death."[44]

These studies, of course, do not by themselves prove that the criminal justice system itself *causes* the high rates of violent death among those youth who are progressively ensnared in it. But they do show that, at best, the system most often fails to stop this grim trajectory. And research increasingly shows why. As we've seen in chapter 4, pervasive mental health and other issues among prisoners are mostly not dealt with, and the surrounding conditions in the neighborhoods to which they return once they leave custody are unlikely to have changed, at least not for the better.[45] For the most part, people who come out of jail, youth detention, or adult prison have both the greatest needs and the least help, and face the most imposing obstacles to stability and security—meaning that they fail often and quickly, falling back to the bottom of the ladder in a society where the bottom is extraordinarily far down by comparison with other advanced industrial societies. It is thus disheartening, but not entirely surprising, that people released from our state prisons get arrested again an average of five times each over the course of the following nine years, with 83 percent of those released getting re-arrested at least once during that period.[46]

We've attempted to deal with this predictable dynamic mostly through what has so far been a very limited set of programs. Some of these are promising, some are not—but the best ones have never been mounted on anything approaching the scale that would be required to make much of a difference in the lives of most young people who pass through the system, and they are routinely foiled by the adverse conditions that lie in wait for prisoners when they are released—what the criminologist Alessandro De Giorgi describes as "widespread public neglect, institutional indifference, and programmatic abandonment."[47] A commitment to full employment and the rebuilding of the public sector offers a way out of this self-defeating cycle of criminal justice involvement, failed "reintegration," and repeated violence in two main ways. First, it could greatly expand the help we are able to offer those who come out of our prisons and jails, by consistently providing the resources to train and hire people who can work effectively with a deeply troubled population that requires concentrated and careful attention—a population beset by drug and alcohol problems, family difficulties, illiteracy, and, often, formidable mental health issues. (In the study of youth sent to a juvenile detention center in Chicago, the researchers found that almost two-thirds of male and three-fourths of female delinquents in their sample had at least one identifiable psychiatric disorder; the Flint Youth Study similarly found that roughly 50 percent of young people involved in gun-related violence had at least one psychiatric diagnosis.)[48] Second, a national commitment to job creation would mean that there are real opportunities for former prisoners to earn a livelihood—as opposed to the vague hope that, with a little advice on how to look for jobs and write résumés, they will manage to "transition" into a "regular" labor market whose central problem is that it is not regular at all.

But even providing better services and opportunities for released prisoners won't be sufficient if we continue incarcerating great numbers of mostly impoverished Americans for long stretches of time and then try to pick up the pieces after we have helped to break them. The strong evidence that mass incarceration is itself destructive both for individuals and communities tells us that we need to admit that this experiment was a failure, and commit ourselves to a different vision of how we respond to people who break the law. That has begun to happen already, at least in modest ways, and the reversal of decades of relentlessly rising imprisonment in the last few years has been a welcome change. But it's far too early to conclude, as some have, that we're witnessing the "end" of mass incarceration.[49] Since its height in 2007, our state and federal prison population has fallen by about 6 percent, or roughly 93,000 people in an overall prison population of more than 1.4 million.[50] The decline has left us, so far, with an incarceration rate about what it was in 1997—when we had already quadrupled it over the course of twenty-five years. And there will continue to be high numbers of people behind bars as long as our efforts to reduce imprisonment continue to focus almost entirely on minor offenders. Many states and the federal system, for example, have moved to release low-level drug offenders early, or to keep them out of secure custody in the first place; that is surely a step in the right direction, and it has helped to reduce the human and fiscal costs of incarceration without increasing crime. But fully 60 percent of black offenders in America's state prisons (versus about 48 percent of whites) are behind bars for a violent offense.[51] Their numbers grew so dramatically after the 1970s in large part because we instituted harsher and more frequent prison sentences for violent crimes while largely ignoring the need to address the social deficits that produced them. If we really want to roll back our counterproductive resort to imprisonment in enduring and significant ways, we will have to change our approach to that population as well.

One strategy, proposed by Yale law professor James Forman Jr. and legal reform advocate Sarah Lustbader, is to develop teams within the courts to review existing sentences for serious offenders—particularly older prisoners who have already served many years and are well past the age at which most people commit violent crimes—and to release those who pose no real threat to the community.[52] We can couple that with work at the "front end" of the criminal justice system, investing more resources into proven programs that provide youths who have committed violent offenses with intensive help to deal with the problems that got them into trouble. The evidence suggests that well-designed and well-implemented programs of this kind can help to put many youth on a better track and keep them out of prison.[53] But the effects will only last if the track actually leads somewhere. Here again, a national commitment to full employment, backed by fully funded public investment in social programs, can make a crucial difference—and in the process do much to transform our criminal justice system. If we provide resources to hire and train more people who are capable of giving guidance to young offenders, we kill two birds with one stone: we provide youth with timely help toward a better future, *and* we see to it that there is a better future to help them into.

It might be objected that a radical reduction in incarceration is a utopian idea. But for decades America had far lower incarceration rates than we do now, while suffering less violence. And it's important to remember that most of the rest of the advanced industrial world manages violence much better than we do while maintaining rates of imprisonment that run anywhere from one-third to one-sixteenth of ours.[54] That difference is partly a result of our unusually high rate of serious crime, especially violent crime.[55] But it also reflects long-standing differences in social values. Many of our counterparts in the advanced industrial world have adopted attitudes toward imprisonment that mesh with their more generous and inclusive social policies in general—and thus, to a greater extent than the United States, avoid the destructive mistake of substituting punishment for constructive strategies of social inclusion and support.[56] Our commitment to the prison as a first-line solution to violence, in short, reflects the same neglectful and exclusive mentality that has encouraged our high rates of violence in the first place.

There is considerable (and welcome) debate about what role, if any, prison should play in a civilized society. But there is a growing recognition that maintaining our current levels of imprisonment is socially and economically self-defeating and morally unsustainable. Bringing them down to a level that is compatible with a democratic and humane society cannot be achieved overnight, but it should be an aspiration—part of a larger vision of the kind of inclusive and supportive society we would like to become. We might start, for example, by committing to the goal of reducing our national incarceration rate to its level in the late 1960s, before the prison boom began in earnest. Or we might aim to reduce our incarceration rate to the average among other advanced industrial societies, which would give us a rate something like one-sixth of our current one. But, again, we can't really envision serious reductions in incarceration as a credible policy option without a simultaneous commitment to the construction of alternative lives and strengthened communities.

V

It is hard to overstate the role of guns in facilitating violent death and injury in black America. Eighty-three percent of black Americans who died by violence in 2018 died by gunshot. The figure climbs to 86 percent for black men specifically, and to an astonishing 94 percent for black men aged fifteen to twenty-nine.[57] And these proportions have been increasing in recent years. Guns did not start the crisis of endemic violence, but beyond a certain point the saturation of communities by firearms becomes an independent force that intensifies and lethalizes it. The glut of guns, as the research makes clear, fuels a deadly self-perpetuating dynamic: an environment where many people carry guns and are known to be willing to use them will breed defensive gun carrying in response. In the worst case, retaliation in kind against gun assault becomes regarded as mandatory in order to maintain the respect that could forestall repeat victimization later on. In the Flint youth violence study, nearly a quarter of youth who presented to the emergency room for *any* kind of assault reported possessing a firearm in the past six months. And this group was much more likely than other assaulted youth to "endorse aggressive attitudes that increase their risk for retaliatory violence."[58]

Substantially changing that dynamic, and more generally reducing the role of guns in these communities, through gun regulation alone—especially through the generally mild measures that are most often proposed by gun control advocates in the United States—is not as easy as it might seem. Decades of stunningly lax gun policies have allowed vulnerable communities to be flooded with guns for so long that even if we managed to stop the flow of new guns tomorrow, we would still be left with a formidable and entrenched arsenal. And some common proposals, though certainly reasonable, are too narrow to have more than a limited impact on "everyday" violence. Restricting the sale of semiautomatic assault rifles, for example, or banning bump stocks and other particularly egregious enhancements of the destructive capacity of firearms, would surely be a good thing—but the vast majority of violent gun deaths and injuries among black Americans, as among all Americans, are inflicted by handguns.

At least two gun control measures, however, are especially urgent. One is closing the "loophole" that in many states allows private gun sales to proceed without a background check; the other is restricting the number of guns that can be bought at one time. Both of these would directly address some of the key sources of the relentless flow of guns into the most affected communities.

At this writing, only about twenty states and the District of Columbia have laws on the books that require background checks for all gun sales.[59] This means that in most states of the union, anyone, no matter what their background or what criminal activities they are engaged in, can buy a firearm—at a gun show, in a personal sale between private parties, or on the Internet. An estimated 22 percent of gun buyers across the United States now buy their weapons without undergoing a background check, and the figure rises to 50 percent for those who purchase their guns in private sales.[60] Unsurprisingly, research shows that this is how a very substantial proportion of guns used in crimes find their way to the street. Closing this "loophole"—less a loophole than a wide-open gate—is absolutely essential: it makes a mockery of our already limited efforts to regulate commercial gun sales in the United States.

Similarly, only a handful of states now have any regulations whatever on bulk gun purchases, and in most of them, such as California, the limit still allows the purchase of one gun a month. Any measure with the potential to reduce the flow of guns into vulnerable communities even slightly is surely better than nothing, but a one-gun-a-month law still allows someone bent on doing violence to arm a dozen of their friends every year. A more substantial step has been taken by New York City, which now allows one gun purchase every ninety days. That is still a lot of guns. But if this approach were implemented nationally, it could have a real impact on what is now a virtually unfettered flow of guns into the communities most vulnerable to firearm violence. And we could certainly make the limit even stricter.

Turning these and other relatively modest local measures into *national* policy is absolutely essential. Currently, even the best efforts of individual states and cities are routinely undercut by the near-total absence of intelligent firearm policies in other places that may be, at most, only a few hours away by freeway. Research shows clearly that guns used in crimes in states with relatively strong gun restrictions are more likely to have come from outside the state than the guns used in crimes in more lax states.[61] Four states—Virginia, Georgia, North Carolina, and South Carolina—supply nearly half of the guns recovered in crimes in New York City, which, like many other major American cities, has relatively stringent gun regulations. Sixty percent of guns used in Chicago crimes come from out of state, with more than one-fourth from Indiana and Mississippi alone. Mississippi, indeed, has the dubious distinction of being, proportionately, the foremost exporter of guns used in crimes committed in other states.[62] There is simply no way to keep Mississippi guns out of Chicago in the absence of a federal policy that makes guns hard to buy in Mississippi. And the same holds for the problem of private gun sales: California's law mandating background checks for all private sales won't stop a handgun bought at an Arizona gun show from quickly winding up on the streets of East Oakland.

Taking these very basic steps should be seen as no more than a beginning. They would still not bring us close to the more mindful gun policies of most other advanced nations; and they would not, by themselves, eliminate racial disparities in violent death and injury. But they are critical first moves that could help tamp down the tragic cycle of defensive weapon carrying and retaliatory violence that plays a role in creating them.

VI

Reducing counterproductive incarceration and the flow of guns can be seen as methods of harm reduction, strategies that would work alongside the kinds of social investment that violence-torn communities most need. Another kind of harm reduction involves efforts to directly counter the destructive attitudes that are often fostered by structural disadvantage and the experience of entrenched violence itself. We cannot sugarcoat the long-term psychological impact of generations of racial subordination, constricted opportunities, and entrenched violence. As we've seen, that experience can lead, at the extreme, to markedly heedless, opportunistic, and individualistic perspectives on the world. And for many young people now trapped in an environment of hopelessness and pervasive danger, it is difficult to imagine a different way of life. Interviewing violent youth confined in New York City's Rikers Island jail, for example, researchers found that most had a "very sophisticated understanding" of the roots and consequences of the violence that enveloped their lives. They also understood that by continuing to engage in it, they were "contributing to an endless cycle that would result in further imprisonment, lack of opportunity, and community disintegration." But despite that awareness, they "could not envision another way of surviving."[63]

As observers from John Dollard onward have recognized, violence directed inward, into one's own community, can be seen in part as a response to this absence of a sense of alternatives. But enlisting youth in the work of social reconstruction holds the promise of genuine personal transformation. Working with young people to build a sense of common purpose, solidarity, and common vision may go a long way toward reshaping what is now too often a predatory, defensive, and "hard" worldview, which sees others as targets and is quick to define them as implacable enemies rather than people much like themselves.[64] We cannot realistically hope to transform those perspectives in the long run without altering the conditions that bring them about—especially the deep poverty, vanished opportunities, and absence of social support for the young. But we can accomplish a great deal by enlisting youth themselves in that process of change. And nothing is more likely to offer that kind of community engagement than guaranteeing youth the opportunity to work in projects designed to create social and environmental reforms that directly affect their lives.

As we've seen, this idea was central to Kenneth Clark's approach to delinquency and youth violence. In the process of transforming their communities, he believed, young people could also transform themselves. Clark saw this as an alternative to the way that conventional social service agencies approached the treatment of young people, focusing on their deficiencies rather than their potential and seeing them as problems rather than resources. Half a century later, it is still true that too much of what we now do in the name of "intervening" with vulnerable youth consists of trying to teach them to adapt to intolerable conditions—to accept uncomplainingly the prospect of lives that are dramatically different from those of more fortunate people, and that offer little hope of anything much better. The evidence tells us that that approach is more often futile than not. But focusing on youths' potential can give us a new and empowering vision of what it means to intervene with young people at risk.

Fortunately, a number of grassroots youth-serving organizations have been working to put this kind of vision into practice in communities across the United States. As my colleagues Tim Goddard and Randy Myers have shown, these programs often aim to raise young people's awareness of the social forces that have damaged their communities and stunted their futures, and mobilize them in the service of projects that challenge those forces.[65] Like many creative efforts at social change in struggling communities, most of these programs operate on a shoestring budget and cope with routine uncertainty about their ability to keep functioning. We need more of them—more interventions based on inspiration and critical thinking rather than on coercion and fear—and we need stable funding to allow them to do their best work. Here again, a commitment to public investment in job creation could make all the difference.

A related approach involves taking advantage of existing strengths within vulnerable communities to create alternative strategies for public safety—strategies that could partly make up for the inability or unwillingness of formal law enforcement to reliably provide it. The 2020 protests against abusive policing have driven home the reality that, since the Jim Crow era, police have not only failed to reliably protect black Americans against violence in their communities but, all too often, have contributed to it. This doesn't mean that there aren't dedicated efforts by some police departments to build respectful and empathic relationships with violence-torn communities, and it is important to support these.[66] It does mean that there are fundamental reasons why people who live in those communities often do not trust police and do not believe that they will be reliably protected by them—or from them. However well-trained and professional police officers may be, at the end of the day they have been put in the position of containing the consequences of an essentially exploitative and discriminatory social order.[67]

In this context, community-based security strategies that draw on the unique strengths of residents themselves offer one promising alternative. This is especially true of efforts to counteract the spiraling cycles of assault and retaliation that have been found again and again to be a crucial factor in the persistence of violent injury and death. In interviews with former gang members now working to defuse gang violence in Los Angeles, for example, Charlotte Bradstreet found that they were often able to achieve a level of street credibility and rapport with gang youth that formal agencies could not match, and that this frequently enabled them to successfully avert what might have been escalating warfare. But she also found that this work was difficult to sustain: though it was challenging and often dangerous, it provided at best only a bare-bones, uncertain livelihood for the men who put themselves on the line to do it.[68] As with involving youth in community action, investing more substantially in this kind of peacemaking would tackle two needs at once: it could provide steady and meaningful work and a solid income for people who are hard to employ because of their past justice system involvement, and it could provide tangible public safety benefits in communities torn by violence.

VII

The public social investments I've called for are not cheap, and it is reasonable to ask where the money to pay for them will come from. There are at least three compelling answers. One we've touched on already. Though the kinds of public investments that I'm proposing do call for large outlays in the beginning, all of the evidence tells us that even from the simplest economic perspective, they pay off over time. This is mainly because they substitute productive spending— spending that builds human capacities and reduces the inequalities that erode them—for reactive, compensatory spending aimed at containing the consequences of our failure to invest in people. What most people forget when they ask where the money is going to come from is that we are already spending it, just in the wrong ways. We spend it, grudgingly, to support people who are involuntarily out of work. We spend it to incarcerate people at a rate unmatched by any other nation on the planet. We spend even more in the productivity lost when we systematically thwart the potential economic contributions of great numbers of people forced to the margins of society. And, of course, we spend it on violence itself. In Chicago alone, according to one estimate, gun violence costs around $2.5 billion a year—in medical and public safety expenses, lost earnings and taxes, and more.[69]

In short, inequality, especially on the level that we tolerate it in America, is expensive. Joblessness is expensive. Alienation and hopelessness are expensive. And violence is expensive. The savings we stand to gain from reversing these long-standing social deficits by putting people to work in socially useful tasks are immense, almost incalculable over time. But we are like the shortsighted homeowner who continually puts off fixing a leak in the basement because it "costs too much"—and then is faced with staggering repair bills when the foundation of the house begins to crumble.

Another part of the answer is that America's $20 trillion economy has more than enough money available to meet these needs; the issue is that we are virtually unique among advanced industrial countries in our unwillingness to tap it to confront our most critical—and costly—social problems. Of the thirty-five other countries in the Organisation for Economic Co-operation and Development, only a handful devote a smaller proportion of their GDP to public spending than we do—mainly much poorer countries like Turkey, Mexico, and Chile.[70] Our tax system, while slightly progressive overall, both takes in less than those of most other advanced countries and grants extraordinary leniency to forms of income (including inheritance and income passively derived from wealth, such as capital gains) that are heavily concentrated among the rich, who not coincidentally tend disproportionately to be white. In the top 1 percent of American income earners, 90 percent are non-Hispanic whites; just 4 percent are black. At the other end of the income distribution, the picture is reversed: black and Latino households are one and a third times more likely to be in the bottom 60 percent than white households are.[71]

Recent changes in the tax laws, as a report from the Center on Budget and Policy Priorities exhaustively details, have only reinforced these racial disparities in taxation. In 2018, 24 percent of the total tax savings resulting from the Trump administration's tax reforms of the previous year went to white households in the top 1 percent of earners, while just 14 percent of the savings went to the entire bottom 60 percent of households of all races.[72] All told, it's estimated that these racially inequitable tax cuts will cost the Treasury close to $2 trillion over the course of a decade—money that could pay for a dramatic transformation of our poorest communities. And they come on top of years of prior depletion of public social spending.

But there is yet another, even more basic answer to the question of where the money for social investments is going to come from. We need to stand the question on its head and ask, instead, where America's money came from in the first place. We are one of the richest societies in the world, and our wealth did not appear from nowhere: it came in part from exploiting the labor and resources of the people who are now in most need of help.

There is considerable debate today about how, as a society, we can best repay black Americans' economic losses—losses that began with slavery and that continued through the era of Jim Crow right down to the present age of postindustrial austerity and neglect. Most of the strategies I've discussed in this chapter are, on the surface, racially neutral. They are designed to provide, as a matter of right, the things that all Americans of all races most need to flourish, now and in the future: meaningful work; a steady and adequate income; the kind of health care that only the better-off can now afford; an education that inspires, builds capacities, and opens opportunities; and—not least—freedom from unjust punishment and the threat of official violence. But when we commit to supporting these fundamental human needs fully and universally, at the level that our resources make possible, we automatically distribute the benefits most heavily to those who have the greatest need and who have made the largest sacrifices. In practice, then, these universal strategies are far from neutral in their potential impact on racial inequality.

Many people feel that such policies, by themselves, aren't enough, and that we also need race-specific approaches that more directly confront the historic theft of wealth—actual and potential—from black Americans. For the first time in many years, this debate has reached the level of congressional dialogue, with the House of Representatives convening a historic hearing in 2019 on reparations for slavery and the subsequent history of systematic discrimination.[73] As of this writing, parallel bills have been launched in the House and Senate to establish a commission to study these issues, and a similar bill to create the country's first state-level task force on reparations has just passed the California state assembly.

These are important developments, and long overdue. But reparations and social investments are complementary, not conflicting. I do not think that we can end the extreme poverty and marginalization that predictably breed violence over the long term without committing ourselves to permanent, universal strategies of public investment aimed at reducing inequality and increasing opportunity and social support. At the same time, a concurrent commitment to providing compensation for the wealth historically taken from black Americans could also help to close the wide gap in opportunities that racial disparities in wealth have created—providing resources for college education, homeownership, business development, and more. Determining the specifics of a meaningful reparations strategy—how much America owes, how to pay for it—is a work in progress.[74] But committing ourselves to exploring the question at the national and state levels is a crucial first step.

VIII

The central message of this book is that there is nothing normal or inevitable about the racial divide in violent death and injury that continues to haunt America. It is the product of deliberate choices—choices that have systematically privileged some people while systematically depriving others. We have had plenty of opportunities to make different ones. One came during Reconstruction, when we saw the stirrings of a movement to create economic security and political equality for the formerly enslaved. Another came during and after World War II, when unprecedented prosperity created a window of opportunity to extend the benefits of rising productivity to everyone. Both opportunities were mostly squandered. We have another one now, at a time when the country's wealth is at once enormous, growing, and distributed in shockingly unequal ways.

But there are signs that we may already be on the road to squandering this chance as well. The odd paradox of strident demands for austerity in the midst of unprecedented wealth threatens not only to slow the halting advances we've made in improving the lives of the most disadvantaged Americans but to reverse them. As I write, the current administration has moved in many ways to sharpen already extreme inequalities of race and class in the United States: launching, as I've noted, tax cuts that promise to shift trillions of dollars to the wealthy; moving to redefine the federal government's poverty measure in ways that will shrink the availability of a broad range of public benefits to poorer Americans; restricting access to Supplemental Nutrition Assistance (SNAP) benefits for several hundred thousand low-income people; and working to undermine the gains in health-care access achieved through the Obama administration's Affordable Care Act.[75] All of these policies, and similar ones that may be in the wings, have the potential to worsen what are already grim and often deteriorating conditions in the nation's poorest places. We've seen that it is in precisely these communities that violent death and injury have been most intractable and, in some cases, increasing in recent years. No one can predict whether the continuing drain of resources from those communities will further increase the level of violence in the future. But it would be a mistake to bet against it.

If we do squander this opportunity—if we continue to tolerate the conditions that breed needless death, injury, and fear, even though we possess both the knowledge and the resources to end them—there is a very good argument that we will be in violation of widely recognized human rights. Article 3 of the Universal Declaration of Human Rights, adopted by the United Nations in 1948, establishes that "everyone has the right to life, liberty, and security of person." Article 22 makes clear that this right is not abstract, but that everyone "as a member of society" is "entitled to realization" of "the economic, social, and cultural rights indispensable for [their] dignity and the free development of [their] personality." The responsibility for that realization is clear: it is to come through "national effort" and in "accordance with the organization and resources of each State." Article 23 specifies that these rights include the "right to work" and to "protection against unemployment," as well as "just and favorable remuneration" than will ensure for individuals and their families "an existence worthy of human dignity." And article 25 elaborates on "the right to a standard of living adequate for the health and well-being" of individuals and families, which includes "housing and medical care and necessary social services," as well as security against unemployment, sickness, and "other lack of livelihood" in circumstances beyond their control.[76]

A follow-up agreement, the International Convention on the Elimination of All Forms of Racial Discrimination, adopted in 1965, specifically guarantees these rights "without distinction as to race, colour, or national or ethnic origin." It singles out, among others, the right to "security of person and protection by the State against violence or bodily harm, whether inflicted by government officials or by any individual, group or institution."[77] These global agreements, then, not only establish a fundamental and universal right to conditions that make for well-being, dignity, and security—including protection against violence— but also make it clear that societies have a responsibility, within the limits of their resources, to keep their members safe and allow them to thrive. By these standards, we are clearly failing.

W.E.B. Du Bois called out that failure—that egregious gap between possibility and reality—more than a century ago:

> Other centuries looking back upon the culture of the nineteenth would have a right to suppose that if, in a land of freemen, eight millions of human beings were found to be dying of disease, the nation would cry with one voice, "Heal them!" If they were staggering on in ignorance, it would cry, "Train them!" If they were harming themselves and others by crime, it would cry, "Guide them!"

Those cries, he said, "are heard and have been heard in the land." But they had "ever been drowned out by counter-cries and echoes: 'Let them die!' 'Train them like slaves!' 'Let them stagger downward!'"

Du Bois acknowledged that "the problems are difficult, extremely difficult." But they were "such as the world has conquered before and can conquer again." And he concluded:

> If in the heyday of the greatest of the world's civiliza-
> tions, it is possible for one people . . . [to] slowly mur-
> der [another] by economic and social exclusion . . . if the
> consummation of such a crime be possible in the twenti-
> eth century, then our civilization is vain and the republic
> is a mockery and a farce.[78]

FURTHER READING

I've necessarily gone very quickly—too quickly—over many things that are important to an understanding of the roots of violence in black America. Some of them involve historical developments—the history of segregation and deindustrialization, for example. Others involve particular topics that I was only able to touch on briefly but that call for much more exploration. Here I want to list just a few sources for those who may want to explore that background further.

The work of the most insightful black scholars of the twentieth century has been shamefully neglected, and some of them are only now beginning to get the attention they deserve. W.E.B. Du Bois's *The Souls of Black Folk* remains a classic and eloquent statement that has much to teach us today. David Levering Lewis's *W.E.B. Du Bois: A Biography* (New York: Henry Holt, 2009) illuminates both Du Bois's own life and work and the turbulent

social context in which he lived—and which he helped to transform. Aldon D. Morris's *The Scholar Denied: W.E.B. Du Bois and
the Birth of Modern Sociology* (Oakland: University of California
Press, 2015), as the title indicates, explores the systematic marginalization of Du Bois and his work within the world of established social science. David A. Varel's *The Lost Black Scholar:
Resurrecting Allison Davis in American Social Thought* (Chicago:
University of Chicago Press, 2018) similarly illuminates the
multiple professional and personal obstacles faced by the highly
respected coauthor of *Children of Bondage* and, in the process,
tells us a great deal about the depth and endurance of the resistance to diversity in white academia.

There is a vast literature on the history of race and racism
in America, but I've found several key works to be nearly indispensable. Eric Foner's *A Short History of Reconstruction* (New York:
Harper, updated edition 2015) remains a concise and illuminating discussion of the short-lived promise of that era. Leon Litwack's stunning *Trouble in Mind: Black Southerners in the Age of
Jim Crow* (New York: Knopf, 1998) is more than a thorough history of the era: it is a compelling human document that helped
to shape my own understanding of the meaning of American
history. Douglas Blackmon's *Slavery by Another Name: The Re-
Enslavement of Black Americans from the Civil War to World War II*
(New York: Doubleday, 2008) provides a wrenching account
of the capture of Southern "justice" by corporations looking for
cheap labor, heedless of black lives in the process. Both books
help to illuminate the violent backdrop to the work of the pioneering scholars of racial disparities in violence in the first half of
the twentieth century.

A number of recent and not-so-recent works are vital in
charting the emergence and growth of segregation and racial-

ized disadvantage across the United States. Several books have described the long-standing racial divide in the provision of social benefits in America; the most powerful is Michael K. Brown's *Race, Money, and the American Welfare State* (Ithaca, NY: Cornell University Press, 1999). The pervasive history of deliberate segregation of American communities through housing policy has recently been detailed in Richard Rothstein's *The Color of Law: A Forgotten History of How Our Government Segregated America* (New York: Liveright, 2017). Thomas J. Sugrue's *The Origins of the Urban Crisis: Race and Inequality in Postwar Detroit* (Princeton, NJ: Princeton University Press, 2005) is a classic analysis of deindustrialization and decline in the United States in the twentieth century, seen through the lens of one of the most devastatingly affected cities in the country. William Julius Wilson's *When Work Disappears: The World of the New Urban Poor* (New York: Vintage Books, 2011) analyzes the impact of the destruction of livelihoods across the United States in recent years and suggests the prescience of some of the observers of race and the American economy from the 1940s through the 1960s. Michael K. Brown et al.'s *Whitewashing Race: The Myth of a Color-Blind Society* (Berkeley: University of California Press, 2003; I am among the coauthors of this book) challenges the idea that discrimination no longer mattered much at the start of the twenty-first century by assessing the evidence across many realms of American life, from the economy to schooling to criminal justice. The evidence of the country's failure to fulfill the hopes of twentieth-century reformers is brought up to date in Fred Harris and Alan Curtis's *Healing Our Divided Society: Investing in America Fifty Years After the Kerner Report* (Philadelphia: Temple University Press, 2018). William A. Darity Jr. and A. Kirsten Mullen's *From Here to Equality: Reparations for Black Americans in the Twenty-First*

Century (Chapel Hill: University of North Carolina Press, 2020) lays out a comprehensive and detailed case for reparations. And Peter Edelman's *Not a Crime to Be Poor: The Criminalization of Poverty in America* (New York: New Press, 2019) unpacks the many ways in which a net of discriminatory laws helps to perpetuate a deeply racialized American poverty.

I regularly rely on several research and advocacy organizations for essential data and analysis of many of the issues raised in this book. A very short list would include:

On jobs, poverty, economic policy, taxation, and social benefits, as well as health-care and education policy:

- Center on Budget and Policy Priorities (https://cbpp.org)
- Economic Policy Institute (https://epi.org)
- Urban Institute (https://urban.org)

On criminal justice practices, incarceration, intervention programs, and community reconstruction:

- The Eisenhower Foundation (http://eisenhowerfoundation.org)
- Justice Policy Institute (http://justicepolicy.org)
- MDRC (http://mdrc.org)
- The Sentencing Project (https://sentencingproject.org)

NOTES

INTRODUCTION

1. Madeline Buckley, "74 People Shot, 12 Fatally, in Chicago over the Weekend," *Chicago Tribune*, August 6, 2018.
2. Sam Charles, Alexandra Arriaga, Manny Ramos, and Yvonne Kim, "Lives Lost: These Are the Victims of Chicago's Bloodiest Weekend of 2018," *Chicago Sun-Times*, August 10, 2018.
3. Tom Schuba, "Stray Gunfire Leaves 1 Dead, 1 Wounded in Englewood," *Chicago Sun-Times*, August 6, 2018.
4. Charles et al., "Lives Lost."
5. Ibid.
6. In this book I use the terms *black* and *African American* interchangeably—primarily because that is how the terms are most often used in the various literatures that I explore here. But it's important to acknowledge two issues: first, that there is debate about what terminology is most appropriate, and for whom, and many people do draw a distinction between these terms; and second, that the

experiences of various groups that are officially defined as "black" in the United States are not all the same when it comes to the issues this book raises. People whose heritage is from the Caribbean have different histories than black Americans whose ancestors have been in the United States since the time of slavery, and recent immigrants from Africa even more so. There is some research on the impact of these differences, but it does not alter the main thrust of the book's argument.

7. "In Chicago, 355 People Have Been Killed This Year. That Is 117 Fewer Than 2017," *Chicago Tribune*, August 27, 2018.

8. US Census Bureau, *Quickfacts: Chicago, Illinois*, accessed August 25, 2018.

9. My calculations from *Uniform Crime Report, 2016* (Washington, DC: Federal Bureau of Investigation, 2017).

10. Kyle Bentle, Jonathan Berlin, Ryan Marx, and Kori Rumore, "39,000 Homicides: Retracing 60 Years of Murder in Chicago," *Chicago Tribune*, January 9, 2018.

11. Gina Tron, "Lollapalooza Death, Fatal Shooting Spree Mark Dark Weekend in Chicago," Oxygen.com, August 6, 2018.

12. Mitchell Armentrout, "Call for Backup: In Wake of Bloody Weekend, Rahm Vows Hundreds of Extra Cops," *Chicago Sun-Times*, August 8, 2018.

13. Alice Yin, "Most Violent Weekend in Chicago This Year: At Least 52 Shot, 8 Fatally," *Chicago Tribune*, June 3, 2019; Julie Bosman, "7 Killed in Weekend Violence in Chicago," *New York Times*, August 6, 2019.

14. For a fuller discussion of this argument, see Elliott Currie, "Confronting the North's South: On Race and Violence in the United States," *International Journal of Crime, Justice, and Social Democracy* 6, no. 1 (March 2017): 43–59.

15. My calculations from Centers for Disease Control and Prevention, *WISQARS Injury Mortality Report*, accessed July 2019.

16. The possibility that growing inequality will breed growing violence is not abstract: the country's homicide rate increased markedly after 2014, and though the rise took place across all races, it was worst in precisely the kinds of communities that were already the most vulnerable. For an illuminating exploration of these

increases, see Richard Rosenfeld and James Alan Fox, "Anatomy of the Homicide Rise," *Homicide Studies* 23, no. 3 (2019): 202–24.

17. W.E.B. Du Bois, *The Philadelphia Negro: A Social Study* (New York: Schocken Books, 1967 [1899]), 163.

ONE | DIMENSIONS

1. Ebola figures from World Health Organization, cited in Centers for Disease Control and Prevention, 2014–2016 Ebola Outbreak in West Africa, https://www.cdc.gov/vhf/ebola/history/2014-2016-outbreak/case-counts.html.

2. Homicide death figures in this section, unless otherwise noted, are from Centers for Disease Control and Prevention, *WISQARS Fatal Injury Reports, National, Regional, and State, 1981–2018*, https://www.cdc.gov/injury/wisqars/fatal.html.

3. International male homicide rates from World Health Organization, *Age-Standardized Rate per 100,000 Population by Cause, Sex, and WHO Member State, 2016*, GHE2016_Death-Rates—Country-4, accessed August 7, 2019.

4. The rate of homicide death among white men, moreover, has recently been increasing—by 18 percent from 2014 to 2018 alone—perhaps as a by-product of the widespread opioid epidemic. See Rosenfeld and Fox, "Anatomy of the Homicide Rise."

5. Centers for Disease Control, *WISQARS Fatal Injury Reports, National, Regional, and State, 1981–2018*.

6. Top 50 cities list from Citizens' Council for Public Security and Criminal Justice (Mexico), as reported in Christopher Woody, "These Were the Most Violent Cities in the World in 2017," *Business Insider*, March 6, 2018.

7. Race and poverty figures for individual cities from US Census Bureau, *Quickfacts*, accessed October 2017.

8. Baltimore figures from Kevin Rector, "Deadliest Year in Baltimore History Ends with 344 Homicides," *Baltimore Sun*, January 1, 2016.

9. Janet Lauritsen and Theodore Lentz, "National and Local Trends in Serious Violence, Firearm Victimization, and Homicide," *Homicide Studies* 23, no. 3 (2019): 243–61. For Chicago, see Garth Nyambi

Walker, Suzanne McLone, Maryann Mason, and Karen Sheehan, "Rates of Firearm Homicide by Chicago Region, Age, Sex, and Race/Ethnicity, 2005–2010," *Journal of Trauma and Acute Care Surgery* 139, no. 5 (May 2017): 81, and 139, no. 4, supplement 1 (2016): S48–53.

10. Anna J. Dare, Hyacinth Irving, Carlos Manuel Guerrero-Lopez, Leah K. Watson, Patrycja Kolpak, Luz Myriam Reynales Shigematsu, Marcos Sanches, David Gomez, Hellen Gelband, and Prabhat Jha, "Geospatial, Racial, and Educational Variation in Firearm Mortality in the USA, Mexico, Brazil, and Colombia, 1990–2015: A Comparative Analysis of Vital Statistics Data," *Lancet Public Health* 4, no. 6 (June 2019): e281–90.

11. Caitlin A. Farrell, Eric W. Fleegler, Michael G. Monuteaux, Celeste R. Wilson, Cindy W. Christian, and Lois K. Lee, "Community Poverty and Child Abuse Fatalities in the United States," *Pediatrics* 139, no. 5 (May 2017): 1–9.

12. Abdulrahman M. El-Sayed, Darryl W. Finkton Jr., Magdalena Paczkowski, Katherine M. Keyes, and Sandro Galea, "Socioeconomic Position, Health Behaviors, and Racial Disparities in Cause-Specific Infant Mortality in Michigan, USA," *Preventive Medicine* 76 (July 2015): 8–13.

13. Emiko Petrosky, Janet M. Blair, Carter J. Betz, Katherine A. Fowler, Shane P. D. Jack, and Bridget H. Lyons, "Racial and Ethnic Differences in Homicides of Adult Women and the Role of Intimate Partner Violence—United States, 2003–2014," Centers for Disease Control and Prevention, *Morbidity and Mortality Weekly Report*, July 21, 2017.

14. Catherine G. Velopulos, Heather Carmichael, Tanya L. Zakrison, and Marie Crandall, "Comparison of Male and Female Victims of Intimate Partner Homicide and Bidirectionality—an Analysis of the National Violent Death Reporting System," *Journal of Trauma and Acute Care Surgery*, April 1, 2019. A study using similar data, but focusing on Chicago and several Illinois counties, found that blacks were 62 percent of victims of intimate partner homicide, non-Hispanic whites 21 percent: Sana Yousuf, Suzanne McLone, Maryanne Mason, Lisa Snow, Carol Gall, and Karen Sheehan, "Factors Associated with Intimate Partner

Homicide in Illinois, 2005–2010: findings from the Illinois Violent Death Reporting System," *Journal of Trauma and Acute Care Surgery* 83, supplement 2 (November 2017): S217–21. See also, for Wisconsin, Kirsten M. Beyer, Peter M. Leyde, L. Kevin Hamberger, and Puroshottam W. Laud, "Does Neighborhood Environment Differentiate Intimate Partner Femicides from Other Femicides?" *Violence Against Women* 21, no. 1 (2015): 49–64.

15. The following figures are calculated from Centers for Disease Control and Prevention, *WISQARS Fatal Injury Reports, Leading Causes of Death Reports, 1981–2018*, https://www.cdc.gov/injury/wisqars/fatal.html.

16. These and the following figures are from Centers for Disease Control and Prevention, *WISQARS Fatal Injury Reports, Years of Potential Life Lost (YPLL) Report, 1981–2018*, https://www.cdc.gov/injury/wisqars/fatal.html.

17. Anthony L. Bui, Matthew M. Coates, and Ellicott C. Matthay, "Years of Life Lost Due to Encounters with Law Enforcement in the USA, 2015–2016," *Journal of Epidemiology and Community Health* 72, no. 8 (August 2018): 715–18.

18. On the impact of improved medical intervention on homicide and its measurement, see, for example, Anthony R. Harris, Steven H. Thomas, Gene A. Fisher, and David J. Hirsh, "Murder and Medicine: The Lethality of Criminal Assault, 1960–1999," *Homicide Studies* 6, no. 2 (May 2002): 128–66. A more recent study finds that, once they do arrive at a trauma center, blacks are somewhat more likely to die of their injuries, even after accounting for differences in severity: Anthony R. Harris, Gene A. Fisher, and Stephen H. Thomas, "Homicide as a Medical Outcome: Racial Disparity in Deaths from Assault in US Level I and II Trauma Centers," *Journal of Trauma and Acute Care Surgery* 72, no. 3 (March 2012): 773–82.

19. For a more detailed discussion of the limits of these measures, see Elliott Currie, *The Roots of Danger: Violent Crime in Global Perspective*, rev. ed. (New York and Oxford: Oxford University Press, 2015), chapter 1.

20. These and the following figures are from Centers for Disease Control and Prevention, *WISQARS Non-fatal Injury Reports, 2000–2017*,

https://www.cdc.gov/injury/wisqars/nonfatal.html, accessed September 2017.

21. Embry Howell, Sam Bieler, and Nathaniel Anderson, *State Variation in Hospital Use and Cost of Firearm Assault Injury, 2010* (Washington, DC: Urban Institute, August 2014).

22. Bindu Kalesan, Stefan Dabic, Sowmya Vasan, Steven Stylianos, and Sandro Galea, "Racial/Ethnic Specific Trends in Pediatric Firearm-Related Hospitalizations in the United States, 1998–2011," *Maternal and Child Health Journal* 20, no. 5 (2016): 1082–90.

23. David C. Moore, Zachary T. Yoneda, Mallory Powell, Daniel L. Howard, A. Alex Jahangir, Kristin R. Archer, Jesse M. Ehrenfeld, William T. Obremskey, and Manish K. Sethi, "Gunshot Victims at a Major Level I Trauma Center: A Study of 343,866 Emergency Department Visits," *Journal of Emergency Medicine* 44, no. 3 (2013): 585–91.

24. David H. Livingston, Robert F. Lavery, Maeve C. Lopreiato, David F. Lavery, and Marian R. Passannante, "Unrelenting Violence: An Analysis of 6,322 Gunshot Wound Patients at a Level I Trauma Center," *Journal of Trauma and Acute Care Surgery* 76, no. 1 (January 2014): 2–11. A study of gunshot wounds from 1996 to 2015 in Memphis, Tennessee, similarly shows both rising numbers of gun assaults overall and increasing severity of injuries: Nathan R. Manley, Timothy C. Fabian, John F. Sharpe, Louis J. Magnotti, and Martin A. Croce, "Good News, Bad News: An Analysis of 11,294 Gunshot Wounds (Gsws) over Two Decades in a Single Center," *Journal of Trauma and Acute Care Surgery* 84, vol. 1 (January 2018): 58–65.

25. Laura Zebib, Justin Stoler, and Tanya Zakrison, "Geo-demographics of Gunshot Wound Injuries in Miami-Dade County, 2002–2012," *BMC Public Health* 17, no. 174 (2017): 1–10.

26. Flint data from Census Bureau, *Quickfacts: Flint City, Michigan*, accessed December 2019.

27. Rebecca M. Cunningham, Megan Ranney, Manya Newton, Whitney Woodhull, Marc Zimmerman, and Maureen A. Walton, "Characteristics of Youth Seeking Emergency Care for Assault Injuries," *Pediatrics* 133, no. 1 (January 2014): e96–e105.

28. Rebecca M. Cunningham, Patrick M. Carter, Megan Ranney, Marc A. Zimmerman, Fred C. Blow, Brenda M. Booth, Jason Goldstick, and Maureen A. Walton, "Violent Reinjury and Mortality Among Youth Seeking Emergency Department Care for Assault-Related Injury: A 2-Year Prospective Cohort Study," *JAMA Pediatrics* 169, no. 1 (2015): 63–70.

29. Patrick M. Carter, Maureen A. Walton, Jason Goldstick, Quyen M. Epstein-Ngo, Marc A. Zimmerman, Melissa C. Mercado, Amanda Garcia Williams, and Rebecca M. Cunningham, "Violent Firearm-Related Conflicts Among High-Risk Youth: An Event-Level and Daily Calendar Analysis," *Preventive Medicine* 102 (September 2017): 112–19.

30. Andria B. Eisman, Quyen M. Ngo, Yasamin Y. Kusonoki, Erin E. Bonar, Marc A. Zimmerman, Rebecca M. Cunningham, and Maureen A. Walton, "Sexual Violence Victimization Among Youth Presenting to an Urban Emergency Department: The Role of Violence Exposure in Predicting Risk," *Health Education and Behavior* 45, no. 4 (August 2018): 625–34.

31. Ibid., 630.

32. Jessica H. Beard, Christopher N. Morrison, Sara F. Jacoby, Beidi Dong, Randi Smith, Carrie A. Sims, and Douglas J. Wiebe, "Quantifying Disparities in Urban Firearm Violence by Race and Place in Philadelphia, Pennsylvania: A Cartographic Study," *American Journal of Public Health* 107, no. 3 (March 2017): 372. Anna Dare and her colleagues found a similar pattern in their comparison of US and Latin American homicides. Young African American men with a college degree or higher suffer nearly triple the firearm homicide rate of white men with a high school education or less, and though the risk of violent death decreases for men of both races as they ascend the scale of education, the racial disparity widens. The best-educated black men have a thirtyfold greater risk of homicide than comparably educated whites; among the less educated, it is only a threefold difference. Dare et al., "Geospatial, Racial, and Educational Variation in Firearm Mortality in the USA, Mexico, Brazil, and Colombia, 1990–2015."

TWO | IMPACTS

1. Carl C. Bell and Esther J. Jenkins, "Traumatic Stress and Children," *Journal of Health Care for the Poor and Underserved* 2, no. 1 (Summer 1991): 176.

2. James Garbarino, Kathleen Kostelny, and Nancy DuBrow, "What Children Can Tell Us About Living in Danger," *American Psychologist* 46, no. 4 (1991): 378.

3. Bell and Jenkins, "Traumatic Stress and Children," 177.

4. Garbarino et al., "What Children Can Tell Us About Living in Danger," 377.

5. Alycia Santilli, Kathleen O'Connor Duffany, Amy Carroll-Scott, Jordan Thomas, Ann Greene, Anita Arora, Alicia Agnoli, Geliang Gan, and Jeanette Ickovics, "Bridging the Response to Mass Shootings and Urban Violence: Exposure to Violence in New Haven, Connecticut," *American Journal of Public Health* 107, no. 3 (March 2017): 374.

6. Ibid., 376–77. See also Albert D. Farrell, Krista R. Mehari, Alison Kramer-Kuhn, and Elizabeth A. Goncy, "The Impact of Victimization and Witnessing Violence on Physical Aggression Among High-Risk Adolescents," *Child Development* 85, no. 4 (August 2014): 1697–99.

7. Tamar Mendelson, Alezandria K. Turner, and S. Darius Tandon, "Violence Exposure and Depressive Symptoms Among Adolescents and Young Adults Disconnected from School and Work," *Journal of Community Psychology* 38, no. 5 (2010): 607–21.

8. Santilli et al., "Bridging the Response to Mass Shootings and Urban Violence: Exposure to Violence in New Haven, Connecticut," 376–77.

9. Garbarino et al., "What Children Can Tell Us About Living in Danger," 379.

10. Janice Johnson Dias and Robert C. Whitaker, "Black Mothers' Perceptions About Urban Neighborhood Safety and Outdoor Play for Their Daughters," *Journal of Health Care for the Poor and Underserved* 24 (2013): 210.

11. Ibid., 210–12.

12. Dexter Voisin, Kate Berringer, Lois Takahashi, Sean Burr, and Jessica Kuhnen, "No Safe Havens: Protective Parenting Strategies for African-American Youth Living in Violent Communities," *Violence and Victims* 31, no. 3 (2016): 523–36.

13. Kerem Shuval, Zohar Massey, Margaret O. Caughy, Brenda Cavanaugh, Charles A. Pillsbury, and Nora Groce, "I Live by Shooting Hill: A Qualitative Exploration of Conflict and Violence Among Urban Youth in New Haven, Connecticut," *Journal of Health Care for the Poor and Underserved* 23 (2012): 135–37.

14. Anne Teitelman, Catherine C. McDonald, Douglas J. Wiebe, Nicole Thomas, Terry Guerra, Nancy Kassam-Adams, and Therese S. Richmond, "Youth's Strategies for Staying Safe and Coping with the Stress of Living in Violent Communities," *Journal of Community Psychology* 38, no. 7 (2010): 7.

15. Ibid., 4.

16. Ibid., 7. See also Dexter R. Voisin, Jason D. P. Bird, Melissa Hardesty, and Cheng Shi Shiu, "African American Adolescents Living and Coping with Community Violence on Chicago's Southside," *Journal of Interpersonal Violence* 26, no. 12 (2011): 2483–98.

17. See Chris L. Gibson, Abigail A. Fagan, and Kelsey Antie, "Avoiding Violent Victimization Among Youths in Urban Neighborhoods: The Importance of Street Efficacy," *American Journal of Public Health* 104, no. 2 (February 2014): e154–e161.

18. Jocelyn R. Smith, "Unequal Burdens of Loss: Examining the Frequency and Timing of Homicide Deaths Experienced by Young Black Men Across the Life Course," *American Journal of Public Health* 105, no. S3 (2015): S483–S490.

19. Ibid., S486–S488.

20. Bell and Jenkins, "Traumatic Stress and Children," 178.

21. Timothy Brezina, Erdal Tekin, and Volkan Topalli, "'Might Not Be a Tomorrow': A Multi-Methods Approach to Anticipated Early Death and Youth Crime," *Criminology* 47, no. 4 (2009): 1113.

22. Ibid., 1115.

23. Ibid., 1116.

24. Bell and Jenkins, "Traumatic Stress and Children," 175–78.

25. Garbarino et al., "What Children Can Tell Us About Living in Danger," 377.

26. Mendelson et al., "Violence Exposure and Depressive Symptoms Among Adolescents and Young Adults Disconnected from School and Work," 612–17.

27. Daisy S. Ng-Mak, Suzanne Salzinger, Richard S. Feldman, and C. Ann Steuve, "Pathological Adaptation to Community Violence Among Inner-City Youth," *American Journal of Orthopsychiatry* 74, no. 2 (2004): 196, 199.

28. Ibid., 206.

29. Sylvie Mrug, Anjana Madan, and Michael Windle, "Emotional Desensitization to Violence Contributes to Adolescents' Violent Behavior," *Journal of Abnormal Child Psychology* 44, no. 1 (2016): 82.

30. Ibid., 82–83. See also Noni K. Gaylord-Harden, Suzanna So, Grace J. Bai, and Patrick Tolan, "Examining the Effects of Emotional and Cognitive Desensitization to Community Violence Exposure in Male Adolescents of Color," *American Journal of Orthopsychiatry* 87, no. 4 (2017): 463–73.

31. Another line of research links exposure to violence and later aggression through the idea that children surrounded by chronic violence may develop "cognitive scripts" that define the world as a hostile place and justify violence as an acceptable response: see, for example, Nancy G. Guerra, L. Rowell Huesmann, and Anja Spindler, "Community Violence Exposure, Social Cognition, and Aggression Among Urban Elementary School Children," *Child Development* 74, no. 5 (September 2003): 1561–76.

32. Garbarino et al., "What Children Can Tell Us About Living in Danger," 378.

33. On this point, see Noni K. Gaylord-Harden, Patrick H. Tolan, Oscar Barbarin, and Velma McBride Murry, "Understanding Development of African-American Boys and Young Men: Moving from Risks to Positive Youth Development," *American Psychologist* 73, no. 6 (2018): 753–67.

34. For a general review of this research, see Anna W. Wright, Makeda Austin, Carolyn Booth, and Wendy Kliewer, "Systematic Review: Exposure to Community Violence and Physical Health

Outcomes in Youth," *Journal of Pediatric Psychology* 42, no. 4 (2017): 364–78.

35. Ibid., 367.

36. Ibid., 373.

37. Ibid.

38. Ibid., 372.

39. Jennifer Ahern, Ellicott C. Matthay, Dana E. Goin, Kriszta Farkas, and Kara E. Rudolph, "Acute Changes in Community Violence and Increases in Hospital Visits and Deaths from Stress-Responsive Diseases," *Epidemiology* 29, no. 5 (September 2018): 684–91.

40. Jessica Galin, Barbara Abrams, Stephanie A. Leonard, Ellicott C. Matthay, Dana E. Goin, and Jennifer Ahern, "Living in Violent Neighborhoods Is Associated with Gestational Weight Gain Outside the Recommended Range," *Pediatric and Perinatal Epidemiology* 31, no. 1 (January 2017): 37–46.

41. Wright et al., "Systematic Review: Exposure to Community Violence and Physical Health Outcomes in Youth," 373–74.

42. Mary Grace Umlauf, Anneliese C. Bolland, Kathleen A. Bolland, Sara Tomek, and John M. Bolland, "The Effects of Age, Gender, Hopelessness, and Exposure to Violence on Sleep Disorder Symptoms and Daytime Sleepiness Among Adolescents in Impoverished Neighborhoods," *Journal of Youth and Adolescence* 44 (2015): 536.

43. Ibid., 519.

44. Ibid., 534. See also Jennifer A. Heissel, Kathryn Grant, Patrick T. Sharkey, Gerard Torrats-Espinosa, and Emma K. Adam, "Violence and Vigilance: The Acute Effects of Community Violent Crime on Sleep and Cortisol," *Child Development* 89, no. 4 (July/August 2018): e323–e331.

45. Bell and Jenkins, "Traumatic Stress and Children," 178.

46. Patrick Sharkey, "The Acute Effect of Local Homicides on Children's Cognitive Performance," *Proceedings of the National Academy of Sciences* 107, no. 26 (June 29, 2010): 11733.

47. Ibid., 11736.

48. Julia Burdick-Will, "Neighborhood Violent Crime and Academic Growth in Chicago: Lasting Effects of Early Exposure," *Social Forces* 95, no. 1 (September 2016): 134.

49. Ibid., 150.
50. Ibid., 153.
51. David J. Harding, "Collateral Consequences of Violence in Disadvantaged Neighborhoods," *Social Forces* 88, no. 2 (December 2009): 765.
52. Ibid., 772.

THREE | EXPLANATIONS, I: PIONEERS

1. Quoted in E. Digby Baltzell, Introduction to the 1967 Edition, W.E.B. Du Bois, *The Philadelphia Negro: A Social Study* (New York: Schocken Books, 1967 [1899]), xix.
2. David Levering Lewis, *W.E.B. Du Bois: A Biography* (New York: Henry Holt, 2009).
3. Du Bois, *Philadelphia Negro*, 311.
4. Ibid., 311–12.
5. Ibid., 238.
6. Ibid., 249.
7. Ibid., 242–43.
8. Ibid., 249.
9. Ibid., 240.
10. Ibid., 241.
11. Ibid., 242.
12. Ibid., 252.
13. Ibid., 254.
14. Ibid., 283.
15. Ibid., 283.
16. Ibid., 284.
17. Ibid., 285–86.
18. Ibid., 323.
19. Ibid., 327.
20. Ibid., 323–24.
21. Ibid., 325.
22. Ibid., 350.
23. Ibid., 351.
24. Ibid.
25. Ibid., 353–54.

26. Ibid., 390.

27. W.E.B. Du Bois, *The Souls of Black Folk*, in *Three Negro Classics* (New York: Avon Books, 1999; originally published 1903), 208–389.

28. Ibid., 218.

29. Ibid., 329–30.

30. Ibid., 330.

31. Ibid., 330–31.

32. Ibid., 332.

33. Ibid., 336.

34. See, for example, Eric Foner, *A Short History of Reconstruction*, updated ed. (New York: Harper, 2015); and also Du Bois's own exploration, *Black Reconstruction in America, 1860–1880* (New York: Free Press, 1998; originally published by Harcourt, Brace in 1935).

35. For a powerful treatment of this period in the South, see especially Leon F. Litwack, *Trouble in Mind: Black Southerners in the Age of Jim Crow* (New York: Vintage Books, 1998). See also Geoff Ward's compelling discussion of the pattern of what he calls "state-organized race crime" against blacks in the Jim Crow era and beyond: Geoff Ward, "The Slow Violence of State-Organized Race Crime," *Theoretical Criminology* 19, no. 3 (August 2015): 299–314.

36. John Dollard, *Caste and Class in a Southern Town*, 3rd ed. (New York: Doubleday Anchor Books, 1957; originally published by Yale University Press in 1937), 1.

37. Allison Davis and John Dollard, *Children of Bondage: The Personality Development of Negro Youth in the Urban South* (New York: Harper and Row, 1964; originally published by the American Council on Education in 1940), 19–20. On the remarkable career of Allison Davis, who among other accomplishments became the first black scholar to gain a tenure-track faculty position at a high-level white university (the University of Chicago, in 1942), see David A. Varel, *The Lost Black Scholar: Resurrecting Allison Davis in American Social Thought* (Chicago and London: University of Chicago Press, 2018).

38. Dollard, *Caste and Class in a Southern Town*, 98.

39. Ibid., 102.

40. Ibid., 174.

41. Ibid., 14.
42. For a recent discussion of this pattern, see Litwack, *Trouble in Mind*, especially 422–28.
43. Dollard, *Caste and Class in a Southern Town*, 267.
44. Ibid., 267–68.
45. Ibid., 268–69.
46. Ibid., 279–80.
47. Ibid., 282.
48. Ibid., 271.
49. Ibid., 274–75.
50. Davis and Dollard, *Children of Bondage*, xx.
51. Ibid., xxi–xxii.
52. Ibid., 20.
53. Ibid., xix.
54. Ibid., xxiv.
55. Ibid., 244–45.
56. Ibid., 247.
57. Ibid., 251.
58. Ibid., 80.
59. Ibid.
60. Ibid., 215.
61. Ibid., 223.
62. Ibid., 225.
63. Ibid., 226–27.
64. Ibid., 270.
65. Guy B. Johnson, "The Negro and Crime," *Annals of the American Academy of Political and Social Science* 217 (September 1941): 93–104.
66. Ibid., 93.
67. Ibid., 99.
68. Ibid., 103.
69. Ibid., 97.
70. Ibid., 101.
71. Ibid.
72. Ibid., 100.
73. Ibid., 103. See the startling discussion of this white attitude toward

black crimes against other blacks in Litwack, *Trouble in Mind*, especially 264–70.

74. Johnson, "The Negro and Crime," 103.

75. Gunnar Myrdal, with the assistance of Richard Sterner and Arnold Rose, *An American Dilemma: The Negro Problem and Modern Democracy* (New York: Harper and Brothers, 1944), 764.

76. Quoted in ibid., 763.

77. Ibid.

78. Ibid., 331–32.

79. Ibid., 332.

80. Ibid., 1003.

81. Ibid., 380.

82. Ibid.

83. Ibid., 1001.

84. Ibid., 1010–11.

85. Ibid., 1021–22.

86. Ibid., 1022–23.

87. Ibid., 382.

88. Ibid., 385.

89. See Walter A. Jackson, *Gunnar Myrdal and America's Conscience* (Chapel Hill and London: University of North Carolina Press, 1990), especially chapter 6.

90. W.E.B. Du Bois, "An American Dilemma," *Phylon* 5, no. 2 (1944): 124.

91. Ralph Ellison, "An American Dilemma: A Review," in *Shadow and Act* (New York: Signet Books, 1966; originally written in 1944), 290–302.

92. Gunnar Myrdal, *Challenge to Affluence* (New York: Vintage Books, 1963).

93. Ibid., 16–17.

94. Ibid., 19.

95. Ibid., 35.

96. Ibid., 35–36.

97. Ibid., 36.

98. Ibid.

99. Ibid., 47.

100. Ibid.
101. Ibid., 66.
102. Ibid., 45.
103. The following pages draw heavily on my collaborative work with Tim Goddard and Randy Myers: see Elliott Currie, Tim Goddard, and Randolph R. Myers, "The *Dark Ghetto* Revisited: Kenneth B. Clark's Classic Analysis as Cutting Edge Criminology," *Theoretical Criminology* 19, no. 1 (February 2015): 5–22.
104. Harlem Youth Opportunities Unlimited, *Youth in the Ghetto: A Study of the Consequences of Powerlessness and a Blueprint for Change* (New York: Harlem Youth Opportunities Unlimited, 1964).
105. Kenneth B. Clark, *Dark Ghetto: Dilemmas of Social Power* (New York: Harper and Row, 1965).
106. Ibid., 81.
107. Ibid., xxii.
108. Ibid., 11.
109. Ibid., 85–86.
110. Ibid., 3.
111. Ibid., 86.
112. Ibid., 89.
113. Ibid., 54.
114. Ibid., 78.
115. Ibid., 101.

FOUR | EXPLANATIONS, II: CONTEMPORARIES

1. National Advisory Commission on Civil Disorders, *Report of the National Advisory Commission on Civil Disorders* (Washington, DC: US Government Printing Office, 1968), 24.
2. Judith R. Blau and Peter M. Blau, "The Cost of Inequality: Metropolitan Structure and Violent Crime," *American Sociological Review* 47 (February 1982): 114–29.
3. Ibid., 119.
4. Ibid., 126.
5. Ibid.
6. Ibid., 119.

7. Ibid.

8. For an early version of the Southern subculture thesis, see Raymond D. Gastil, "Homicide and a Regional Culture of Violence," *American Sociological Review* 36, no. 3 (1971): 412–71; for a rethinking a little over a decade later, see Steven F. Messner, "Regional and Racial Effects on the Urban Homicide Rate: The Subculture of Violence Revisited," *American Journal of Sociology* 88, no. 5 (1983): 997–1007.

9. Marvin Wolfgang and Franco Ferracuti, *The Subculture of Violence: Towards an Integrated Theory in Criminology* (London: Social Science Paperbacks, 1967).

10. Ibid., 298.

11. Ibid., 162.

12. Ibid., 264.

13. Ibid., 298.

14. Ibid., 315.

15. Ibid., 300.

16. Ibid., 312.

17. Lauren J. Krivo, Maria B. Velez, Christopher J. Lyons, Jason B. Phillips, and Elizabeth Sabbath, "Race, Crime, and the Changing Fortunes of Urban Neighborhoods, 1999–2013," *Du Bois Review* 15, no. 1 (2018): 47–68. The study also found that the rising housing instability and mass foreclosures in this period were related to high and growing rates of homicide.

18. Ibid., 52.

19. The link between some measure of "disadvantage" and violence is one of the most consistent in criminology. For a recent review of the international evidence on inequality, poverty, and violence, see Elliott Currie, *The Roots of Danger: Violent Crime in International Perspective* (New York and Oxford: Oxford University Press, 2015), chapter 2. See also Travis C. Pratt and Francis T. Cullen, "Assessing Macro-Level Predictors and Theories of Crime: A Meta-Analysis," in Michael Tonry, ed., *Crime and Justice: A Review of Research* 32 (Chicago: University of Chicago Press, 2005), 373–450.

20. Robert J. Sampson and William Julius Wilson, "Race, Crime, and Urban Inequality," in John Hagan and Ruth D. Peterson, eds., *Crime and Inequality* (Stanford, CA: Stanford University

Press, 1995), 37–54. For a later review of research on these issues, see Ruth D. Peterson and Lauren J. Krivo, "Macrostructural Analyses of Race, Ethnicity, and Violent Crime: Recent Lessons and New Directions for Research," *Annual Review of Sociology* 31, no. 1 (2005): 331–56.

21. Lauren J. Krivo and Ruth D. Peterson, "Extremely Disadvantaged Neighborhoods and Urban Crime," *Social Forces* 75, no. 2 (December 1996): 619–50.

22. Ibid., 620.

23. Ibid., 631.

24. Thomas L. McNulty, "Assessing the Race-Violence Relationship at the Macro Level: The Assumption of Racial Invariance and the Problem of Restricted Distributions," *Criminology* 39, no. 2 (2001): 467–89.

25. Julie A. Phillips, "White, Black, and Latino Homicide Rates: Why the Difference?" *Social Problems* 47, no. 3 (2002): 367.

26. Darrell Steffensmeier, Jeffrey T. Ulmer, Ben Feldmeyer, and Casey T. Harris, "Scope and Conceptual Issues in Testing the Race-Crime Invariance Thesis: Black, White, and Hispanic Comparisons," *Criminology* 48, no. 4 (2010): 1133–69. See also Jeffrey T. Ulmer, Casey T. Harris, and Darrell Steffensmeier, "Racial and Ethnic Disparities in Structural Disadvantage and Crime: White, Black, and Hispanic Comparisons," *Social Science Quarterly* 93, no. 3 (September 2012): 799–819. It's important to note that both Phillips and Steffensmeier and his coauthors stress that the existence of these unexplained forces did not mean that reducing disadvantage would not help to reduce violence.

27. Steffensmeier et al., "Scope and Conceptual Issues in Testing the Race-Crime Invariance Thesis," 1160.

28. Kayla Fontenot, Jessica Semega, and Melissa Kollar, *Income and Poverty in the United States: 2017*, US Census Bureau, Current Population Reports, September 2018. Other recent research that adjusts levels of income to include the effect of social benefits confirms this racial gap in "deep" poverty. As of 2016, black children were roughly two and a half times as likely to be living below half the poverty line as white children (and 40 percent

more likely than Latino children); moreover, their rate of "deep" poverty was higher than it had been in 1995. See Danilo Trisi and Matt Saenz, *Deep Poverty Among Children Rose in TANF's First Decade, Then Fell as Other Programs Strengthened* (Washington, DC: Center on Budget and Policy Priorities, February 27, 2020).

29. Ashley N. Edwards, *Dynamics of Economic Well-Being: Poverty 2009–2011* (Washington, DC: US Census Bureau, January 2014).

30. Julie Siebens, *Extended Measures of Well-Being: Living Conditions in the United States, 2011* (Washington, DC: US Census Bureau, September 2013).

31. For explorations of the particular impact of everyday discrimination on African American crime, see, for example, James D. Unnever and Shaun L. Gabbidon, *A Theory of African American Offending* (New York: Routledge, 2011), and Callie H. Burt, Man Kit Lei, and Ronald L. Simons, "Racial Discrimination, Racial Socialization, and Crime over Time: A Social Schematic Theory Model," *Criminology* 55, no. 4 (November 2017): 938–79.

32. Anita Knopov, Emily F. Rothman, Shea W. Cronin, Lydia Franklin, Alev Cansever, Fiona Potter, Aldina Mesic, Anika Sharma, Ziming Xuan, Michael Siegel, and David Hemenway, "The Role of Racial Residential Segregation in Black–White Disparities in Firearm Homicide at the State Level in the United States, 1991–2015," *Journal of the National Medical Association* 111, no. 1 (February 2019): 62–75.

33. Ibid.

34. Lauren J. Krivo, Ruth D. Peterson, and Danielle C. Kuhl, "Segregation, Racial Structure, and Neighborhood Violent Crime," *American Journal of Sociology* 11, no. 6 (May 2009): 1765–802.

35. Ibid., 1766. A Pennsylvania study similarly shows that whites were more likely to suffer a violence-related injury if they lived in counties with higher levels of racial segregation: Anthony Fabio, Erin K. Sauber-Schatz, Kamil E. Barbour, and Wei Li, "The Association Between County-Level Injury Rates and Racial Segregation Revisited: A Multilevel Analysis," *American Journal of Public Health* 99, no. 4 (April 2009): 748–53.

36. Elizabeth Griffiths, "Race, Space, and the Spread of Violence Across the City," *Social Problems* 60, no. 4 (November 2013): 491–512.

37. Ibid., 509.

38. On this history, see, for example, Michael K. Brown et al., *Whitewashing Race: The Myth of a Color-Blind Society* (Berkeley: University of California Press, 2003); Richard Rothstein, *The Color of Law: A Forgotten History of How Our Government Segregated America* (New York: Liveright, 2017).

39. Sara F. Jacoby, Beidi Dong, Jessica H. Beard, Douglas J. Wiebe, and Christopher N. Morrison, "The Enduring Impact of Historical and Structural Racism on Urban Violence in Philadelphia," *Social Science and Medicine* 199 (February 2018): 87–95.

40. Ibid., 6.

41. Elijah Anderson, *Code of the Street: Decency, Violence, and the Moral Life of the Inner City* (New York: W. W. Norton, 2000).

42. Ibid., 53.

43. Ibid., 285–87.

44. Ibid., 323.

45. Ibid., 286.

46. Ibid., 75.

47. Ibid., 74.

48. Ibid., 66.

49. Ibid., 323.

50. Ibid., 49, 71.

51. Ibid., 289. Using a similar lens, the sociologist Nikki Jones has explored the dynamic of aggression, respect, and retaliation among some African American girls in Philadelphia. "Through observation, instruction, and experience," she writes, "inner-city girls, no less than boys, learn how reputation, respect, and retaliation—the fundamental elements of the code of the street—organize their social world." Nikki Jones, *Between Good and Ghetto: African American Girls and Inner-City Violence* (New Brunswick, NJ: Rutgers University Press, 2010), 6.

52. Joseph B. Richardson Jr., Jerry Brown, and Michelle Van Brakle, "Pathways to Early Violent Death: The Voices of Serious Vio-

lent Youth Offenders," *American Journal of Public Health* 3, no. 7 (2013): e7.

53. Ibid., e8.

54. Ibid., e9.

55. Ibid., e10.

56. Ibid., e14.

57. Ibid., e9. A study of youth incarcerated in New York's Rikers Island jail found many similarities. Youth regarded the ability to use violence effectively as a kind of "capital" that enabled them to achieve a degree of status and security in conditions of pervasive danger where there was little help from outside institutions and, often, little help and much indifference from within their own community as well. This attitude helped to explain the striking severity of the injuries these youth regularly suffered—including a remarkably high number of traumatic brain injuries. "The tough thing is," one youth told the researchers, "when we fight someone, we're doing it to actually hurt them." Jasmine Graves, Jessica Steele, Fatos Kaba, Sarah Glowa-Kollisch, Cassandra Ramdath, Zachary Rosner, Ross MacDonald, Nathaniel Dickey, and Homer Venters, "Traumatic Brain Injury Focus Groups as a Means to Understand Violence Among Adolescent Males in the NYC Jail System," *Journal of Health Care for the Poor and Underserved* 26, no. 2 (2015): 346.

58. Timothy Brezina, Erdal Tekin, and Volkan Topalli, "'Might Not Be a Tomorrow': A Multi-Methods Approach to Anticipated Early Death and Youth Crime," *Criminology* 47, no. 4 (2009): 1113.

59. Ibid., 1117.

60. Ibid., 1118.

61. Robert H. DuRant, Chris Cadenhead, Robert A. Pendergrast, Greg Stevens, and Charles W. Linder, "Factors Associated with the Use of Violence Among Urban Black Adolescents," *American Journal of Public Health* 84, no. 4 (1994): 612–17. A later study of youth in Huntsville, Alabama, found a similar connection between hopelessness and violence: John M. Bolland, Debra

Moehle McCallum, Brad Lian, Carolyn J. Bailey, and Paul Rowan, "Hopelessness and Violence Among Inner-City Youths," *Maternal and Child Health Journal* 5, no. 4 (December 2001): 237–44.

62. Sarah A. Stoddard, Susan J. Henly, Renee E. Sieving, and John Bolland, "Social Connections, Trajectories of Hopelessness, and Serious Violence in Impoverished Urban Youth," *Journal of Youth and Adolescence* 40, no. 3 (2011): 278–95.

FIVE | REMEDIES

1. Valerie Wilson, *Black Unemployment Is at Least Twice as High as White Unemployment at the National Level and in 14 States and the District of Columbia* (Washington, DC: Economic Policy Institute, April 2019).

2. Elise Gould, Julia Wolfe, and Zane Mokhiber, *Class of 2019: High School Edition* (Washington, DC: Economic Policy Institute, June 6, 2019).

3. Matthew D. Wilson and Teresa C. Córdova, *Industrial Restructuring and the Continuing Impact on Youth Employment in Illinois* (Chicago: Great Cities Institute, University of Illinois, May 2018).

4. Teresa C. Córdova and Matthew D. Wilson, *Abandoned in Their Neighborhoods: Youth Joblessness Amidst the Flight of Industry and Opportunity* (Chicago: Great Cities Institute, University of Illinois, January 2017).

5. Matthew D. Wilson, *Out of School and Out of Work: 16 to 19 and 20 to 24 Year Olds in Chicago and Cook County in 2017* (Chicago: Great Cities Institute, University of Illinois, May 2019).

6. Ibid.

7. Wilson and Córdova, *Industrial Restructuring and the Continuing Impact on Youth Employment in Illinois*.

8. Ibid.

9. Gould et al., *Class of 2019: High School Edition*.

10. Mark Paul, William Darity Jr., and Darrick Hamilton, *The Federal Job Guarantee—A Policy to Achieve Permanent Full Employment*

(Washington, DC: Center on Budget and Policy Priorities, March 9, 2018), 9. For a recent elaboration of these ideas, see the podcast "Job Guarantee Now!" with Sarah Treuhaft and Darrick Hamilton, Next System Project, January 2020.

11. Paul et al., *The Federal Job Guarantee—A Policy to Achieve Permanent Full Employment*, 12. The "Green New Deal" resolution proposed in the US Congress in 2019 shares much of this view of the potential and uses of full employment.

12. See, for example, Josh Bivens, "How Do Our Job Creation Recommendations Stack Up Against a Job Guarantee?" Economic Policy Institute, April 12, 2018.

13. Reclaim Our Schools Los Angeles, *Building the Power to Reclaim Our Schools*, Los Angeles, California, July 2019.

14. Michael Leachman, *Many Schools Still Facing Funding Challenges as New Year Starts* (Washington, DC: Center on Budget and Policy Priorities, August 23, 2018). For a useful general analysis of the effects of sharply unequal funding in American schools, see Linda Darling-Hammond, "Education and the Path to One Nation, Indivisible," in Fred Harris and Alan Curtis, *Healing Our Divided Society* (Philadelphia: Temple University Press, 2018), 193–207.

15. See Julie Bosman, "Crumbling, Destitute Schools Threaten Detroit's Recovery," *New York Times*, January 20, 2016.

16. See "Flint Residents Protest Conditions at Southwestern Academy, Other Schools," ABC12 (Detroit), April 30, 2018.

17. Vikki Ortiz, "School Nurses Tackle Mental Health Needs," *Chicago Tribune*, August 26, 2018.

18. Chye-Ching Huang and Roderick Taylor, *Any Infrastructure Package Should Boost Investment in Low-Income Communities* (Washington, DC: Center on Budget and Policy Priorities, April 4, 2019).

19. Elise Gould, Marcy Whitebook, Zane Mokhiber, and Lea J. E. Austin, *Breaking the Silence on Early Child Care and Education Costs: A Values-Based Budget for Children, Parents, and Teachers in California* (Washington, DC: Economic Policy Institute, July 2019).

20. Cited in Parija Kavilanz, "The US Can't Keep Up with Demand for Health Aides, Nurses, and Doctors," CNN Money, May 4, 2018.

21. Steven Ross Johnson, "Report: Public Health Funding Falls Despite Increasing Threats," *Modern Healthcare*, April 24, 2019.

22. Trust for America's Health, *Ready or Not: Protecting the Public's Health from Diseases, Disasters and Bioterrorism, 2019*, 26.

23. Jessie Hellmann, "Coronavirus Poses New Threat for Strained Public Health System," *The Hill*, January 30, 2020.

24. For a general review of research on these job programs, see Elliott Currie, *Crime and Punishment in America*, rev. ed. (New York: Picador, 2013), Afterword, 211–23.

25. Jonathan M. V. Davis and Sara B. Heller, *Policy Brief: One Summer Chicago Plus: Evidence Update 2017* (Chicago: University of Chicago Crime Lab, 2017).

26. Ibid., 5. A recent analysis of several subsidized work programs across the country similarly finds that many private businesses are reluctant to hire the most disadvantaged workers. See Dan Bloom, "Ensuring Equity in Future Subsidized Employment Programs: The Critical Role of Nonprofits, Public Agencies, and Social Enterprises," *Issue Focus* (Washington, DC: MDRC, April 2020).

27. Ibid., 6.

28. For a useful introduction to these programs, see Kelly Field, "Should the U.S. Become a Nation of Apprentices?" *Chronicle of Higher Education*, December 22, 2015; "What Can the U.S. Learn from Switzerland, a World Leader in Apprenticeships?" *Chronicle of Higher Education*, May 2, 2016; and Katherine Mangan, "The Making of a Modern-Day Apprentice," *Chronicle of Higher Education*, June 28, 2017.

29. CareerWise Colorado, https://careerwisecolorado.org, accessed October 2018. The program is being evaluated over the next several years: see MDRC, "CareerWise Colorado: A Modern Youth Apprenticeship Model," podcast, accessed October 17, 2018.

30. Figures on exits from poverty are from the Survey of Income and Program Participation, in Ashley N. Edwards, *Dynamics of Economic Well-Being: Poverty 2009–2011* (Washington, DC: US Census Bureau, January 2014); figures on rates of poverty by employment status are from US Census Bureau, Current Population Reports, *Income and Poverty in the United States: 2016*.

31. David Cooper, "Workers of Color Are Far More Likely to Be Paid Poverty-Level Wages Than White Workers," Economic Policy Institute, Working Economics Blog, June 21, 2018.

32. Elise Gould, "What to Watch on Jobs Day: Public Sector Jobs Are Threatened by Austerity and Attacks on Collective Bargaining," Economic Policy Institute, Working Economics Blog, July 15, 2018.

33. Marcy Whitebook, Marisa Schlieber, Aline Hankey, Lea J. E. Austin, and George Philipp, *Teachers' Voices: Work Environment Conditions That Impact Teachers' Practice and Program Quality—New York* (Berkeley: Center for the Study of Child Care Employment, University of California, 2018), 6.

34. International poverty figures from UNICEF, *Child Well-Being in Rich Countries* (Florence: Innocenti Research Center, 2013). See also Valerie Wilson and Jessica Schieder, *Countries Investing More in Social Programs Have Less Child Poverty* (Washington, DC: Economic Policy Institute, June 1, 2018). For a powerful depiction of extreme poverty in the United States in an international context, see *Report of the Special Rapporteur on Extreme Poverty and Human Rights on His Mission to the United States of America* (United Nations, General Assembly, Human Rights Council, May 2018).

35. Heather L. Sipsma, Erika Rogan, Lauren A. Taylor, Kristina M. Talbert-Slagle, and Elizabeth H. Bradley, "Spending on Social and Public Health Services and Its Association with Homicide in the USA: An Ecological Study," *BMJ Open* 7 (2017): 1–7.

36. For a general discussion of the rise in prison populations, its sources, and its costs, see Currie, *Crime and Punishment in America*, chapters 2 and 3, and Afterword.

37. For some of these critiques, see Michelle Alexander, *The New Jim Crow: Mass Incarceration in the Age of Colorblindness* (New York: New Press, 2012); Marc Mauer, *Race to Incarcerate*, rev. ed. (New York: New Press, 2006); and Currie, *Crime and Punishment in America*.

38. Elliott Currie, "Race, Violence, and Criminal Justice," in Harris and Curtis, *Healing Our Divided Society*, 308.

39. Ibid., 309.

40. Current African American imprisonment rates from Jennifer

Bronson and E. Ann Carson, *Prisoners in 2017* (Washington, DC: US Bureau of Justice Statistics, April 2019).

41. Georgina Sturge, Briefing Paper, *UK Prison Population Statistics*, UK House of Commons Library, July 23, 2019.

42. For a review of the literature on these negative impacts, see Currie, *Crime and Punishment in America*, 195–202; for specific analyses, see Steven Raphael and Michael A. Stoll, *Do Prisons Make Us Safer?: The Benefits and Costs of the Prison Boom* (New York: Russell Sage, 2009); and for a classic analysis of the adverse community impact of mass imprisonment, see Todd Clear, *Imprisoning Communities: How Mass Incarceration Makes Disadvantaged Neighborhoods Worse* (New York: Oxford University Press, 2009).

43. Linda A. Teplin, Gary M. McClelland, Karen M. Abram, and Darinka Mileusnic, "Early Violent Death Among Delinquent Youth: A Prospective Longitudinal Study," *Pediatrics* 15, no. 6 (June 2005): 1586–93.

44. Matthew C. Aalsma, Katherine S. L. Lau, Anthony J. Perins, Katherine Schwartz, Wanzhu Tu, Sarah E. Wiehe, Patrick Monahan, and Marc B. Rosenman, "Mortality of Youth Offenders Along a Continuum of Justice System Involvement," *American Journal of Preventive Medicine* 50, no. 3 (2016): 303–10.

45. For a recent study of these issues in Massachusetts, see Bruce Western, *Homeward* (New York: Russell Sage, 2019).

46. Nine-year arrest figures from Marion Alper, Matthew DuRose, and Joshua Markman, *2018 Update on Prisoner Recidivism: A 9-Year Follow-up Period (2005–2014)* (Washington, DC: US Bureau of Justice Statistics, May 2018).

47. Alessandro De Giorgi, "Back to Nothing: Prisoner Reentry and Neoliberal Neglect," *Social Justice* 44, no. 1 (2017): 92.

48. Teplin et al., "Early Violent Death Among Delinquent Youth: A Prospective Longitudinal Study," 1591. For a recent review of research showing the many obstacles to effective mental health treatment for African American youth, see Arrianna M. Planey, Shardé McNeil Smith, Stephanie Moore, and Taylor D. Walker, "Barriers and Facilitators to Mental Health Help-Seeking Among African American Youth and Their Families:

A Systematic Review Study," *Children and Youth Services Review* 101 (2019): 190–200.

49. For a critical analysis of the limits of these recent reforms, see Sonya Goshe, "The Limits of Criminal Justice Reform," in Walter S. DeKeseredy and Elliott Currie, eds., *Progressive Justice: Strategies for Change in an Age of Repression* (London: Routledge, 2019).

50. Danielle Kaeble and Mary Cowhig, *Correctional Populations in the United States, 2016* (Washington, DC: US Bureau of Justice Statistics, April 2018).

51. Ibid.

52. James Forman Jr. and Sarah Lustbader, "Rethinking Extreme Sentences," *New York Times*, August 2, 2019. An analysis by the Justice Policy Institute estimates that Maryland's recent release of 192 elderly long-term inmates could save the state roughly $1 billion in prison costs without a significant impact on public safety. *Rethinking Approaches to Over Incarceration of Black Young Adults* (Washington, DC: Justice Policy Institute, November 2019), 9.

53. For research evidence on the effectiveness of "front end" programs to keep violent youth out of prison, see Currie, *Crime and Punishment in America*, 76–106, 207–23.

54. For current national incarceration rates around the world, see International Centre for Prison Studies, *World Prison Brief*, at www.prisonstudies.org/world-prison-brief-data.

55. Allen J. Beck and Alfred Blumstein, "Racial Disproportionality in Us State Prisons: Accounting for the Effects of Racial and Ethnic Differences in Criminal Involvement, Arrests, Sentencing, and Time Served," *Journal of Quantitative Criminology* 34 (2018): 853–83.

56. An illuminating analysis of this meshing of prison policy and wider social priorities in the Nordic countries can be found in John Pratt and Anna Eriksson, *Contrasts in Punishment* (Abingdon, UK, and New York: Routledge, 2011).

57. Figures from Centers for Disease Control and Prevention, *WISQARS Fatal Injury Reports*, accessed March 2020.

58. Patrick M. Carter, Maureen A. Walton, Manya F. Newton, Michael Clery, Lauren K. Whiteside, Marc A. Zimmerman, and Rebecca M. Cunningham, "Firearm Possession Among Adolescents Presenting

to an Urban Emergency Department for Assault," *Pediatrics* 132, no. 2 (August 2013): 213–21.

59. Data from Giffords Law Center, https://lawcenter.giffords.org, accessed October 2018.

60. Matthew Miller, Lisa Hepburn, and Deborah Azrael, "Firearm Acquisition Without Background Checks: Results of a National Survey," *Annals of Internal Medicine* 166, no. 4 (February 2017): 233–39.

61. E. J. Olson, M. Hoofnagle, E. J. Kaufman, C. W. Schwab, P. M. Reilly, and M. J. Seamon, "American Firearm Homicides: The Impact of Your Neighbors," *Journal of Trauma and Acute Care Surgery* 86, no. 5 (2019): 797–802.

62. Chicago gun imports from Shibani Maktani, "Report Finds Most Guns Used in Chicago Crimes Come from Outside City," *Wall Street Journal*, October 29, 2017. New York gun sources from Philip Bump, "Where the Guns Used in Chicago Actually Come From," *Washington Post*, November 7, 2017.

63. Jasmine Graves, Jessica Steele, Fatos Kaba, Sarah Glowa-Kollisch, Cassandra Ramdath, Zachary Rosner, Ross MacDonald, Nathaniel Dickey, and Homer Venters, "Traumatic Brain Injury Focus Groups as a Means to Understand Violence Among Adolescent Males in the NYC Jail System," *Journal of Health Care for the Poor and Underserved* 26, no. 2 (2015): 353.

64. For a more detailed discussion of this issue, see Elliott Currie, "Consciousness, Solidarity, and Hope as Prevention and Rehabilitation," *International Journal of Crime, Justice, and Social Democracy* 2, no. 2 (2013): 3–11.

65. Tim Goddard and Randy Myers, *Youth, Community, and the Struggle for Social Justice* (Abingdon, UK: Routledge, 2017).

66. There is some evidence that the presence of police review boards may diminish violence in cities, other things being equal: see María B. Vélez, Christopher J. Lyons, and Wayne A. Santoro, "The Political Context of the Percent Black–Neighborhood Violence Link: A Multilevel Analysis," *Social Problems* 62, no. 1 (February 2015): 93–119.

67. For a penetrating discussion of this point, and a related critique of current proposals for police reform, see Alex Vitale, *The End of Policing* (New York: Verso, 2017).

68. Charlotte Bradstreet, "Life on the Line: An Exploration of Street Outreach and Gang Prevention and Intervention Work in Los Angeles" (unpublished PhD diss., University of California, Irvine, 2015).

69. Cited in Córdova and Wilson, *Abandoned in Their Neighborhoods: Youth Joblessness Amidst the Flight of Industry and Opportunity*, 2.

70. Chye-Ching Huang and Roderick Taylor, *How the Federal Tax Code Can Better Advance Racial Equity* (Washington, DC: Center on Budget and Policy Priorities, July 25, 2019), 11.

71. Ibid., 9.

72. Ibid., 22. Further lobbying efforts have added several hundred billion dollars more to these highly skewed losses: see Jesse Drucker and Jim Tankersley, "Business Got Big Tax Cut: Lobbyists Made It Bigger," *New York Times*, December 31, 2019.

73. Sheryl Gay Stolberg, "A Historic Hearing on Slavery, and the Struggle That Remains," *New York Times*, June 20, 2019.

74. For a range of views on these issues, see Michael T. Martin and Marilyn Yaquinto, eds., *Redress for Historical Injustices in the United States: On Reparations for Slavery, Jim Crow, and Their Legacies* (Durham and London: Duke University Press, 2007). For an insightful recent view, see Ta-Nehisi Coates, "The Case for Reparations," in *We Were Eight Years in Power* (New York: One World, 2017), 163–208. And for a thorough exploration of possible reparation strategies, see William A. Darity Jr. and A. Kirsten Mullen, *From Here to Equality: Reparations for Black Americans in the Twenty-First Century* (Chapel Hill: University of North Carolina Press, 2020), especially chapter 13.

75. Robert Greenstein, *Misguided Trump Administration Rule Would Take Basic Food Assistance from Working Families, Seniors, and People with Disabilities* (Washington, DC: Center on Budget and Policy Priorities, July 23, 2019).

76. United Nations, *Universal Declaration of Human Rights*, December 1948, in *25+ Human Rights Documents* (New York: Center for the Study of Human Rights, Columbia University, 2005), 5–7.

77. *Convention on the Elimination of All Forms of Racial Discrimination*, United Nations, December 1965, in ibid., 39.

78. Du Bois, *Philadelphia Negro*, 387–88.

ACKNOWLEDGMENTS

I'd like to thank the team at Metropolitan Books, including Sara Bershtel, Grigory Tovbis, and Janel Brown, for their support and careful work on this project, which made what can be a grueling experience altogether enjoyable and made this a better book.

I doubt that I could have even contemplated writing this book without the strong foundation given to me as a graduate student by the late Robert Blauner, who taught a deeply informative course on race and ethnic relations at the University of California, Berkeley, for many years. Bob knew the research and theory in the field backward and forward, and he demanded that his students take seriously the work that had gone before us.

What I think of as my second graduate education on issues of race and social justice took place when I worked with an extraordinary group of coauthors—Michael Brown, Martin Carnoy, Troy Duster, David Oppenheimer, Marjorie Shultz, and David Wellman—to write the book *Whitewashing Race: The Myth of a Color-Blind Society*, which appeared in 2003. My ongoing conversations with David Wellman have enriched my thinking on these issues—and many others—ever since.

The list of friends, students, and colleagues who have helped me to think about social issues gets longer and longer, and I'll just single out a few for now: Frank Cullen, Walter DeKeseredy, Bob Dunn, Dave Fogarty, Hardy Frye, Dan Maier-Katkin, Henry Pontell, and Diego Vigil. Jerome Skolnick's friendship and support have buoyed me since I was a graduate student and provided an ongoing lesson in how to do creative social science in the service of justice. Alan Curtis, who has truly walked the walk when it comes to turning good ideas into action, has taught me more than I can say about the real work of social change. Thanks also to Maura Roessner for early support of this project.

Working with my former students, now colleagues, Tim Goddard and Randy Myers has been deeply rewarding, and I hope they'll forgive me for liberally borrowing, in chapter 3 of this book, from our joint writing on the work of Kenneth B. Clark. In addition to that article, which appeared in the journal *Theoretical Criminology* in 2015, some of the ideas developed here appeared earlier in *The Palgrave Handbook of*

Criminology and the Global South, *Contexts*, the *International Journal of Crime, Justice, and Social Democracy*, and *Healing Our Divided Society: Investing in America Fifty Years After the Kerner Report*, edited by Fred Harris and Alan Curtis. I also presented some of these ideas, in earlier form, in several places, including the International Conference on Crime, Justice, and Social Democracy in Brisbane, Australia (thanks to Kerry Carrington and her staff); the annual conference of the American Society of Criminology (twice; thanks to Randy Myers and Alan Curtis); the Department of Sociology at the University of Tennessee, Knoxville (thanks to Lois Presser and Michelle Brown); the Department of Criminology at the University of West Georgia (thanks to Gavin Lee and Lynn Pazzani); the Luskin School of Public Affairs at the University of California, Los Angeles (thanks to Mark Kaplan); the Department of Criminology and Criminal Justice at Northern Arizona University (thanks to Ken Cruz); and at Social Justice Week at Sonoma State University (thanks to Diana Grant, Bryan Burton, and Anastasia Tosouni).

Finally, I'd like to be sure my family knows that they have been the source of inspiration and purpose for everything I've written: Rachael Peltz; Sonia Peltz-Currie; David Sandy; Susannah, John, Luke, Henry, and Lucy Maddock; and Carolyn Currie.

INDEX

ABOUT THE AUTHOR

ELLIOTT CURRIE is the author of *Crime and Punishment in America*, which was a finalist for the Pulitzer Prize, and of numerous other acclaimed works on crime, juvenile delinquency, drug abuse, and social policy. He is a professor of criminology, law, and society at the University of California, Irvine, and an affiliate of the School of Justice, Faculty of Law, at Queensland University of Technology in Australia.